Jack Altman

Contents

This Way Jordan		**3**
Flashback		**7**
On the Scene		**15**
Amman		
and the Jordan Valley		**15**
Eastern Desert		**31**
Around the Dead Sea		**33**
Petra to Aqaba		**39**
Cultural Notes		**52**
Shopping		**54**
Dining Out		**57**
Sports		**59**
The Hard Facts		**60**
Index		64

Fold-out map

Jordan, Amman,

Petra, Jerash,

Aqaba

This Way Jordan

Adventurous travellers drawn to Jordan soon make the acquaintance of the ghosts of the past. This is a land that has been crisscrossed throughout the centuries by nomads and biblical prophets, merchants of the exotic, and conquering armies of Romans, Byzantines, Arabs, Crusaders and Ottoman Turks. In their wake have been left such splendours as the Nabataean city of Petra carved from the desert rock, or the beautifully preserved Roman city of Jerash 50 km (30 miles) north of Amman.

After feasting on such sights, the bedazzled modern visitor can easily change pace by relaxing for a while at a beach resort on the Gulf of Aqaba or going on a shopping spree in a Thousand and One Nights Arab bazaar.

Valley, Dead Sea and Desert

Jordan extends east from the fertile valley of the Jordan river and the Dead Sea to the deserts of Arabia that cover two-thirds of the country's 89,200 sq km (34,400 sq miles). The land shares borders with Syria to the north, Iraq and Saudi Arabia to the east and Israel to the west, including the West Bank of the Jordan river that has been occu-pied by the Israelis since the 1967 war and is now being progressively ceded to the Palestinians.

The Jordan Valley is part of the Great Rift Valley that starts up in Syria and ends in Mozambique. It constitutes the country's only arable land, producing wheat, barley, citrus fruits, figs, apricots, apples, grapes, olives, aubergines and tobacco, and its great need for irrigation water remains a major issue in its relations with neighbouring Israel and Syria. It is also a place of religious significance for many creeds, being the place where Jesus was baptised and the Prophet Mohammed crossed over from Mecca to the Dome of the Rock.

The Jordan river flows into the Dead Sea, the deepest part of the Rift Valley and indeed the lowest point on earth—400 m (1,300 ft) below sea level, with its own sea bed another 300 m deeper. Its high saline content—26 per cent compared with normal seawater's 3 to 4 per cent—means not only that you can't sink but also that nothing can live in it. The Dead Sea region produces potash for export and bitumen, much valued since the time of the pharaohs when it served in the process of mummification. The southern tip 3 of the Dead Sea is also the land of the legendary sinful cities of Sodom and Gomorrah, where Lot's wife was turned to a pillar of salt—there is plenty of salt, to be sure, but no trace of the cities.

Today's major towns command the heights above the valley. Half the country's industries are based in the capital Amman, with a population estimated around 2 million. It is flanked by Salt, Zarqa, Ajlun, Irbid and Jerash to the north, and Madaba, Karak, Petra, Ma'an and Aqaba to the south.

The desert to the east and southeast of the Jordan Valley is a sprawling upland plateau that was divided in biblical times into the lands of Ammon, Moab and Edom. In the desolate hinterland are the ruins of fortresses built by the Romans to protect their trade routes and later, in the 8th century, revamped by the Umayyad Arabs: the once-mighty Mushah, Amra, Shawmari and Azraq. In modern times, the desert was the stage upon which the dashing Lawrence of Arabia carried out his sorties with the Bedouin to thwart their Ottoman rulers in World War I.

Cutting their way west to the Jordan river and Dead Sea, the desert *wadis*, or dry river beds, of Yarmuk, Zarqa (Yabbok in the Bible), Mujib (Arnon), Karak and Hasa (Zered) fill with water only when their steep and narrow gorges are engulfed with flash floods in winter. The Edomite mountains at the southern end of the plateau, east of Aqaba, rise to the country's highest point at Jebel Rum, 1,754 m (5,755 ft).

While the fertile Jordan Valley is understandably filled with flowers in spring—daisies, poppies and hyacinths bloom among the orchards, wheatfields and vineyards—you shouldn't be surprised to see wild flowers in the desert, too. After the winter rains, the desert plateaux around the *wadis* come alive with white broom, pink and purple oleander, juniper, tamarisk and thorny acacia. The thyme and sage used in cooking and the mint in the tea grow wild.

The People

Jordan's population of 5.7 million is mostly a mixture of Palestinians and Arab Bedouins. The former are currently a majority, in large part refugees of the Arab-Israeli wars. Their ancestry goes back beyond the 7th-century Arab conquest to the Philistines of biblical times, to whom they owe their name. There are also small minorities of Armenians and Circassians, originally from the Russian Caucasus. Some 92 per cent of Jordanians are Sunni Muslims, with a small group of Druze practising a dissident form of Islam, and 6 per cent Christian, mostly Greek Orthodox.

Apart from those who have settled down in the towns in recent times, many of the Bedouin —meaning "desert-dwellers" in Arabic—can be spotted near their distinctive long, black, goat-hair tents erected in the sands or grazing their flocks of goats and sheep in the valley pastures. To the distress of romantics, their camels are increasingly being replaced by Toyota trucks or Mercedes limousines. Bedouin land is divided into mutually acknowledged tribal spheres "occupied" by roving family groups, a community of equals headed by a sheikh.

The Bedouin who continue the nomadic way of life remain fiercely proud of their traditions and tend to be somewhat suspicious of others. Nonetheless, obedience to the cardinal laws of hospitality means they would never betray any open contempt. Visitors will be most courteously invited to take tea or coffee with the men—and carefully watched by the women through a slit in the curtain that separates them.

CAMELS, ONE HUMP OR TWO?

The single-humped camel is more properly known as a dromedary— the *Camelus dromedarius*, renowned "ship of the deserts" of Arabia and North Africa. Sturdy as it is, it cannot handle the extremes of hot and cold nor negotiate steep slopes as does the two-humped Bactrian camel, *Camelus bactrianus*, that roams the steppes of Central Asia. Thanks to the qualities of the Bactrian, say the historians, the Turks, who favoured the two-humped beast, were able to extend their empire much further into colder, mountainous regions than the Arabs, who (with the exception of Spain and southwestern France, which were conquered on horseback) kept largely to the desert lowlands.

The hump on the dromedary is a storage place for protective fat. Its colour may range from off-white to dark brown. At the end of that long neck is—despite the flirtatious double row of eyelashes to fend off sand and wind—a frankly not very pretty face, featuring small ears, tough-skinned lips and powerful teeth, some of them viciously pointed for fighting. The cloven hoofs are broad, flat and thick-soled, preventing the animals from sinking into the sand. Horny pads on chest, knees and thighs provide protection for hard, rocky sleeping surfaces. Like thoroughbred horses, the more slender beasts are bred for speed, while sturdier ones can carry up to 270 kg (600 lb).

Flashback

Beginnings

Jordan's story as a separate nation is of very recent vintage, starting with the post-colonial 20th century. Prior to that, its fortunes were conditioned by the geographical position of the Jordan Valley as a land corridor between Asia and Africa. The region was never home to a civilization that could compare to its neighbours all around, but it was the constant beneficiary of their commerce—and unwitting victim of their wars.

Stone Age men and women roamed that corridor long before the merchants and soldiers of recorded history. Archaeologists have excavated the hunters' flint weapons and the bones of their prey—boar, buffalo and elephant —dating back over 200,000 years. At that time, a savannah of trees, long grass and brush covered much of what is now Jordan's eastern desert.

Along with more refined tools and utensils, bones have been found in sufficient quantity in a *wadi* near Petra to suggest that people started herding goats here from about 20,000 BC. Some 10,000 years later, farmers appeared in the Jordan Valley with their first dwellings of round wood and stone huts, and implements for grain-harvesting. These findings have placed "Jordanians" squarely in the Syrian-Palestinian geographical area of the Middle East's Fertile Crescent, which launched agriculture from its base in Mesopotamia. Two of the world's oldest excavated villages (about 7200 BC) have been found at Beidha, near Petra, and Ain Ghazal, near Amman, along with small domestic shrines with statues of deities, and remains of tall earthenware jars used for storing oil, wheat and barley.

In the 4th millennium BC, copper was mined at Feinan north of Petra and later alloyed into bronze to be used for tools and jewellery. Writing arrived from Mesopotamia with the region's first merchants by about 3200 BC.

Biblical Times

To the extent that the Bible can be considered a historical chronicle as well as a work of spiritual revelation, Jordan made its entrance into history hand in hand with Israel. Scanty archaeological

Bedouin tea time. The people of the desert are renowned for their courteous hospitality.

evidence suggests that Sodom and Gomorrah may have been two of the five "Cities of the Plain" in the Valley of Siddim at the southern end of the Dead Sea, identifiable with Bab ed-Dhra, Numeira, as-Safi, Feifeh and Khanazir. They were probably destroyed by invading Amorites in 2300 BC and telescoped by legend to associate them with the arrival of Abraham and Lot in Canaan, several centuries later.

From 1500 to 1200 BC, the Jordanian region was annexed by the Egyptian empire, embroiled in the power struggles of Ramses II and Tuthmosis III with the Mitanni and Hittites in Syria and Palestine. An Egyptian border post appears to have been set up at Tell as-Sa'idiyah in the northern Jordan Valley.

Around 1200 BC, the country was invaded by the "Peoples of the Sea" from the western Mediterranean. These included the Philistines, who may have been Minoan refugees from Crete. Other invaders, according to the Bible, were Hebrews migrating from Egypt. The Hebrews, led by Moses and Joshua, were kept out of Edom (southern Jordan) and camped in the plain of Moab north of the Dead Sea. Moses is said to have climbed Mount Nebo to view the land west of the Jordan river that the Israelites were to conquer.

In the face of this aggressive new nation, the Transjordan (east of the Jordan river) kingdoms of Ammon, Moab and Edom were weakened by the squabbling of their chieftains and reduced to vassal states by the Israelites' king David. The hostility of the three states to his son Solomon prompted their alliance in 930 BC, enabling them in turn to exploit the division of the Jews into the two states of Israel and Judah. The Moabite king Mesha scored an important victory over the Israelites around 850 BC. Ammon and Moab united, but the Edomites continued their separate nomadic life until late in the next century, carrying on a profitable trade in such luxury goods as perfumes, spices and frankincense. But freedom was short-lived, with the region reeling under the conquests of the Assyrians (8th century BC), the Babylonians of King Nebuchadnezzar (605–562 BC) and the Persians of Emperor Cyrus (539 BC).

The Nabataeans arrive, and the Romans

With the conquest of the Persian Empire by Alexander the Great and his early death in 323 BC, the Jordanian region went up for grabs as his Macedonian and Greek generals fought over the territorial spoils. Jordan fell to the Ptolemies ruling from Alexandria, and was then annexed by the Seleucid king, Antiochus III, after he defeated Ptolemy III in 198 BC.

During this period of almost perpetual warfare, a formidable band of semi-nomadic merchants, the Nabataeans, set up a kingdom at the southern end of the Jordan Valley. First mentioned in Assyrian texts of the 8th century BC, they left Arabia some 400 years later to build a splendid desert capital at Petra. They acquired considerable wealth from trading in the luxury goods of gems and silks from India, perfumes and spices from Arabia and in the more mundane—but very lucrative—bitumen from the Dead Sea.

By the 3rd century BC, they had expanded their commercial empire up to Hauran on the Jordanian-Syrian border, westward into the Negev and Sinai deserts, and south of Edom down into Arabia, establishing a port on the Red Sea at Leuke Kome. In their heyday, from the 1st century BC to the 1st century AD, they possessed more than a thousand trading posts throughout the eastern Mediterranean. By then, they were operating under the suzerainty of Rome, Pompey having annexed Syria in 64 BC and captured Petra, but leaving the Nabataean rulers in place.

Major prizes of the Roman conquest were the ten Hellenistic cities of the Decapolis league in the north Jordan Valley, which included Philadelphia (Amman), Gerasa (Jerash), Pella and Gadara (modern Umm Qais). They had thrived under the Seleucids and the Jewish kings of the Hasmonaean (Maccabee) dynasty, and the Romans now developed them further as prosperous centres of cosmopolitan culture.

The Nabataeans continued in quiet, prosperous cooperation until their last king, Rabbel II, died in 106 AD. The Roman emperor

DON'T MESS WITH OUR MYRRH

As Antigonus, King of Macedonia, discovered, the Nabataeans were fierce in the defence of their property. They made their first important appearance on the world stage in 312 BC, when Antigonus sent troops to raid their stores of silver, frankincense and myrrh, left untended during a religious festival. According to an account by the 1st century BC historian Diodorus Siculus, the Nabataeans caught up with the patrol and retrieved their treasure, killing most of the culprits. They sent a furious note with the survivors warning Antigonus not to try that kind of underhanded trick again.

Saladin conquered Shobak castle from the Crusaders and left the Arabic inscriptions on the walls.

Trajan peacefully dissolved the kingdom, dispersing Nabataean troops to the remotest provinces of the Roman Empire. He built a new road down to the Red Sea, the Via Nova Traiana, in order to strengthen the already lucrative trade route. Forts were set up every 20 km as protection against nomadic Arab raiders.

Christianity and Islam

For 13 centuries, Jordan was witness to almost non-stop religious drama and conflict, from the birth of Christianity to the holy wars of Islam and the massacres of the Christian Crusades. The region's involvement in the birth of Christianity began with the pivotal moment when Jesus came down from Nazareth to be baptised by John in the Jordan river. Tradition also has it that Salome's dance for the head of John the Baptist took place in King Herod's palace at Mukawir (Machaerus) on the eastern heights above the Dead Sea. The visit in 326 of Helen, mother of Emperor Constantine, to Jerusalem in search of the True Cross launched a series of pilgrimages by Byzantine Christians to the Jordan Valley— the veritable beginning of the region's tourist trade. From the 6th century, the first churches were built in and around Madaba.

Fatally weakened by its violent clashes with the Persians during the 6th and 7th centuries, the Byzantine Empire was unable to protect Syria, Palestine and the Jordan Valley against the northern advance of Muslim Arabs in 633. By 636, decisive Arab victories over the Byzantine army at Pella and on the Yarmuk river brought the whole region under Islamic rule. Over the next 300 years, Muslims and Christians lived in relative harmony, since the caliphs were more concerned with the power struggles of their Umayyad, Abbasid and Fatimid dynasties. Their infighting in turn left them powerless to resist the new invaders, Seljuk Turks who swept across Asia Minor to capture the region in the last quarter of the 11th century.

The Crusades, during which the Europeans captured Jerusalem in 1099, imposed Christian rule for two centuries in Palestine, much of Syria, and the region the Crusaders referred to as *Oultrejourdain* (Transjordan). Baudouin of Boulogne, King of Jerusalem, led a reconnoitring expedition down the valley in 1115. He built fortresses near Petra, most notably at Shobak (named Montréal by the Crusaders), at Aqaba (then Aila), and later at Karak, southeast of the Dead Sea. Founded to protect the Crusaders' eastern flank and trade routes to the Red Sea, these Jordanian outposts served as bases for the murderous raids of their overlord Renaud de Châtillon, until Saladin, Sultan of Egypt, led the Islamic reconquest in the

THE VILLAIN OF KARAK

Of the Crusades' many villains, none was more notoriously cruel and rapacious than Renaud de Châtillon, who ruled over Transjordan from his castle at Karak. He once smeared honey on a Greek Orthodox patriarch's wounds and left him to the ants until he handed over his hidden treasure. In shamelessly sacrilegious manner, he breached an agreement negotiated with the Arabs not to plunder merchant caravans—robbing and killing Muslims on their holy pilgrimage to Mecca. Saladin's subsequent retaliatory siege of Karak took place in the course of a wedding feast for Renaud's stepson. In that era of medieval chivalry, Renaud's wife sent the sultan some of the choicest dishes she herself had prepared, and Saladin responded gallantly by ordering his artillery not to fire on the bridal suite. But when Renaud was later captured in battle, the sultan put a stop to the courtesy and personally chopped off the ungodly man's head.

1170s. Aqaba fell, both Karak and Shobak were besieged but held out until shortly after Saladin's decisive victory at Hattin on the Sea of Galilee in 1187. Despite a brief "come-back" by Richard the Lion-Heart, the Crusaders dwindled in strength over the next century and were driven from the Middle East once and for all with the fall of Acre (near present-day Haifa) in 1291.

Ottoman Rule

As the last Crusaders left, a new breed of Turks displaced the Seljuks in Anatolia, the dynasty of Osman I—"Ottoman" to the Western world. Ruling the Middle East from Egypt, the Mameluke sultans held out against them until 1516, at which point Transjordan was absorbed into the Ottoman province of Damascus for the next four centuries. The region stagnated under an increasingly indolent regime. Petra had sunk into oblivion until "rediscovered" in 1812 by a Swiss traveller, Johann Ludwig Burckhardt. Even Aqaba, which had long thrived as transit port for Red Sea trade and for Muslim pilgrims to Mecca, suffered in the 19th century from the opening of faster routes through the Suez Canal and via the Hejaz Railway—completed in 1908—from Damascus through Transjordan to Medina.

With Turkey allied to Germany, Aqaba played a key role in World War I. Ottoman troops there endangered the British position in Egypt, and in 1917 one Lt T. E. Lawrence—better known as Lawrence of Arabia—helped Faisal ibn Hussein's Arab forces to capture the port. The British-sponsored Arab revolt then fought through Transjordan along the Hejaz railway to end Ottoman rule in Damascus.

The Modern Kingdom

After World War I, the British mandate over Palestine included Transjordan until Faisal's brother Abdullah arrived to rule in 1921. Formally recognized two years later as an Emirate, the country was obliged to accept British officers at the head of its army, the Arab Legion. Even after independence in 1946, Britain's John Bagot Glubb—"Glubb Pasha" to the Arabs—remained in command of the army until 1956, when the Suez crisis also ended Britain's close treaty relations with its former protectorate.

King Abdullah's newly independent Transjordan joined the Arab war against the new state of Israel in 1948, capturing eastern Jerusalem and occupying most of the central area west of the Jordan which the United Nations had designated as part of Palestine. In April, 1949, Transjordan changed its name to the Hashemite Kingdom of Jordan, anticipating its annexation a year later of the West Bank territory. The move antagonized Arab neighbours favouring an independent state of Palestine, and most of all the Palestinians themselves. In 1951, one of them assassinated Abdullah during prayers at the Al-Aqsa mosque in Jerusalem.

After Abdullah's son was declared mentally unfit to rule, the throne passed to his 17-year-old grandson Hussein in 1953. With a British education at Harrow and Sandhurst military academy, and an American wife, King Hussein pursued a largely pro-Western policy. He had a hard time steering a moderate course in the face of ardent Arab nationalism and Israeli intransigence. From his grandfather, he inherited the hostility of the Palestinians—and half a million refugees (since grown to a majority of Jordan's total population) from the conquered Palestinian territories.

In the Six Day War of 1967, Hussein's army lost East Jerusalem and Israel occupied the West Bank. Hussein had then to deal with the Palestinian Liberation Organization (PLO), which was using Jordanian bases to launch attacks on Israeli-held territory and provoking Israeli reprisals inside Jordan. In September, 1970, the Jordanian army crushed the Palestinian guerrilla forces, and the following year forced the PLO to leave the country.

Though strengthened domestically by this victory, Hussein was obliged by his Arab allies to cede any claims to the West Bank to a future Palestinian state; he formally relinquished them in 1988.

Glimmer of Peace

Chronic economic difficulties involving dependency on oil from neighbouring Iraq and financial aid from the United States came to a head with the Persian Gulf War of 1991. It effectively shut off both lifelines—and brought thousands of Kuwait's Palestinian migrant workers flocking back to Jordan. Hussein manoeuvred with agility, rescuing his good standing with the Americans by signing a peace treaty with Israel in 1994. This also boosted Jordanian tourism.

The advent of a hard-line Israeli government confronted Jordan with renewed difficulties, both from Palestinians and increasingly militant Jordanians demanding better living conditions. With Hussein's death in February 1999 and the succession of his son Abdullah, surviving—occasionally thriving—amid uncertainty continues to be the name of the game. Since 2003 the government includes, for the first time, a certain number of women. 13

On the Scene

Though Jordan seems to be almost all desert when viewed from the air, it is bordered on the northwest by the fertile green ribbon of the Jordan Valley, and most of the touristic sights are concentrated in this vicinity. Four-wheel-drive vehicles are necessary only for venturing into the desert itself.

AMMAN AND THE JORDAN VALLEY

Amman, Salt, Jerash, Ajlun, Pella, Umm Qais

The bustling capital has all the practical facilities of a modern metropolis—fine hotels and restaurants and good shopping possibilities—making it an ideal base for your excursions around the country (except for Petra, Wadi Rum and Aqaba). North towards the Syrian border, amid the rolling hills of the Jordan Valley, lie Jerash and other ancient sites of the Roman Empire's cities of the Decapolis, and the medieval Arab fortress of Ajlun. To do them justice, count on at least a day for Amman itself and one or two for the north.

Amman

The site of this thoroughly up-to-date city, Jordan's capital since 1921, was first inhabited in the Stone Age, over 9,000 years ago. The early inhabitants occupied the heights of what is now the Jebel al-Qala'a citadel. Known in biblical times as Rabbath Ammon ("great city of the Ammonites"), and for a time owing tribute to Israel's king David, the town was renamed Philadelphia by its 3rd-century BC conqueror Ptolemy II Philadelphus. It was later included by the Romans in the region's Decapolis league and prospered as a commercial centre on the route between Syria and the Red Sea. Under Byzantine rule, it was the seat of the combined diocese of Petra and Philadelphia. After the Arab conquest in the 7th century, it received its modern name of Amman.

The city's location on the plateau east of the Jordan Valley some 800 m (more than 2,600 ft) above sea level means that winters can be remarkably cold. Even the dry, hot summers are eased by cool breezes in the evening. The city and its sprawling suburbs—Amman has spread out from its original seven hills to cover 20 or more—embrace nearly half the country's 5 million-plus population. The historic monuments are few but well worth a leisurely visit, and are easily accessible on and around the old Jebel al-Qal'a citadel. Make sure you save some time to browse around the enticing jewellery shops in the market area at the foot of the hill.

The Citadel

The ancient acropolis rises in three terraces over the west side of the city centre. It encompasses traces of the town in prehistoric, Roman, Byzantine and Islamic times. From the top, you have a grand view of both the archaeological sites on the two upper levels and the modern city below. Ongoing excavations are restoring remains of the Temple of Hercules, built under Emperor Marcus Aurelius (AD 161–180). Several columns have been set back in place in what was once a massive edifice erected around a stretch of bare rock. The spot was probably used for sacrifices in an earlier Ammonite shrine dating back to the 9th century BC.

North of the temple, some of its masonry can be seen recycled in the column bases of a Byzantine church, probably 6th-century, which was destroyed by earthquake, not by invaders. The small basilica's two rows of columns divided the mosaic-patterned nave floor (now covered over for protection) from the stone-paved aisles.

Beyond the Byzantine church, the Umayyad palace was originally built around 720 as residence of the governor of Amman and served subsequent administrations for the next 400 years. To the right of the palace entrance are a small mosque, also of the Umayyad period, and a gigantic round cistern, 16 m (52 ft) in diameter and 5 m (16 ft) deep, that stored rainwater. As they did for the basilica, the Arab conquerors re-used materials from the Roman citadel to build the cistern, notably the sturdy column drums and capitals.

The entrance vestibule to the palace itself, in the form of a Greek cross, supports a reconstructed dome. The two corner chambers flanking the cross's south arm may have been guardrooms. Beyond, a series of courtyards, each lined with individual rooms, are linked by what was originally a Roman colonnaded street. The main residential quarters lie in the far northern corner, grouped around another cruciform, once-domed hall that was probably the *diwan*, or throne room, where the governor held his audiences. Renovation is in progress throughout the complex.

Archaeological Museum

In a small building south of the Umayyad Palace, the well-displayed exhibits of jewellery, pottery and sculpture provide a convenient journey through time. In chronological order, you can see the oldest traces of the Stone Age hunters and their prey found up to now in the Jordan Valley, dating back 100,000 to 250,000 years: large stone hand-axes, blades and scraping tools, along with jawbones and teeth of a wild boar, buffalo and wild horse. From Ain Ghazal on the northeastern outskirts of Amman come several white plaster and clay statues of

---

THE LATE KING HUSSEIN

Born in 1935, Hussein ibn Talal ascended the throne at 17, after the abdication of his father. Having witnessed the assassination of his grandfather King Abdullah in Jerusalem in 1951, he was steeled to the tough tasks ahead—not least as the target himself of a dozen assassination attempts, most of them by Palestinian militants and their supporters. Hussein's masterly tightrope act between opposing forces in the turbulent Arab world earned for his country a prestige and importance out of all proportion to its size and real political or military power.

Inside Jordan, his knack for survival won him the affection and admiration at least of the indigenous Bedouin part of the population. They also approved his attachment to traditional values even as he showed such personal modern tastes as piloting his own jet aircraft and riding a motorbike in the desert. And his religious credentials were impeccable: great-grandson of Hussein ibn Ali, Sherif of Mecca, and thus a direct descendant of Mohammed through the Prophet's daughter Fatima. Hussein's education was emphatically British—Harrow public school and Sandhurst military academy, still the training ground for the Jordanian army that grew out of the British-run Arab Legion. After three brief marriages to the daughters of Egyptian, British and Jordanian families, he settled down with his American wife, Queen Noor, born Elizabeth Halaby. With an architecture degree from Princeton, the queen championed the causes of the environment and the fine arts. Hussein's successor, Abdullah, is the son of his British wife, Antoinette Gardiner.

The monochrome mosaic of modern Amman spreads over the hillsides above the theatre.

what were probably anthropomorphic deities from around 6500 BC—among the world's oldest-known statues of the human form. Ceramic burial urns and frescoes of a ritual procession of masked figures heading for a shrine have been recovered from the Teleilat Ghassul settlement near the Dead Sea (4000 BC).

Antiquities imported by Mediterranean traders from 1500 to 1200 BC include Greek Mycenaean bronze daggers, swords and decorated pottery. From the following era come Ammonite sculpture and Moabite carved stone slabs, including a replica of the famous Mesha Stele, 850 BC,

whose inscription records the Moabite victory over the Israelites—the original is in the Louvre in Paris. Fragments of the Dead Sea Scrolls, found in 1952, are in a separate room.

The Nabataeans' kingdom of Petra is represented by their sculpture, fine painted pottery, bronze and silver coins (4th century BC to AD 106). From Jerash and other towns of the Roman Decapolis come ceramic figurines and delicately fashioned coloured glassware. Jewellery of gold, pearls, lapis lazuli and amethyst illustrates the riches of the Byzantine period up to the Islamic conquest in 636. Because of

18

the Islamic taboo on human representation, ceramics are decorated in geometric and floral motifs or Arabic calligraphy.

Roman Theatre

Carved out of a hillside facing the citadel, the nicely restored 6,000-seat theatre is the best-preserved Roman building of ancient Philadelphia. It was inaugurated during the reign of Marcus Aurelius, around AD 170, an architectural showpiece that had been carefully positioned to avoid blinding the spectators with sunlight. Three bands of seats indicate the ranks of viewers: nobles, closest to the arena, then military, followed by the ordinary people. The theatre is once again in use for open-air theatre, music and dance. It also houses two small museums on either side of the auditorium.

Folklore Museum

In the right wing, this is devoted to traditional Bedouin costumes, craftwork, musical instruments, household goods, tools and a goat-hair tent.

Museum of Popular Traditions

In the left wing, it exhibits jewellery, embroidery and household utensils, and a fine collection of mosaics from 6th-century Byzantine churches in and around Madaba and Jerash.

Forum

In front of the theatre, traces of a colonnade leading down a pedestrians-only street are all that remain of what used to be the ancient city's porticoed shopping and business centre. Covering more than 7,600 sq m (9,000 sq yd), Philadelphia's forum was reputed to have been one of the largest in the Roman Empire.

Odeon

East of the theatre is the newly reconstructed, more intimate 2nd-century odeon, originally roofed and seating about 500 spectators. It is to be used for concerts.

Nymphaeum

Several hundred yards southwest of the theatre, the Romans' monumental fountain was originally an ornate two-storey, colonnaded edifice graced with mosaics and marble statues of water nymphs. Its current reconstruction is intended to give some idea of the extravagance accorded to the town's main water supply in this desert region.

Gold Suq

In the immediate vicinity of the nymphaeum is the town's main bazaar area, noted particularly for the jewellery shops where the price of the gold and silver is determined, at least in part, by your personal bargaining skills.

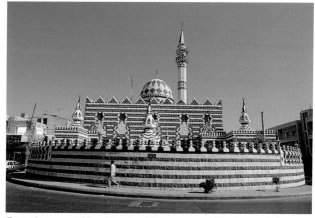

From the eye-catching Abu Darwish mosque, you'll get a good view over the city.

Mosques

Towering above the bazaar are the two minarets of the quarter's landmark, the Hussein Mosque built in the 1920s by Emir Abdullah and restored by his grandson, King Hussein. The foundations of the Ottoman-style building date back to the town's first mosque erected by Caliph Omar ibn al-Khattab in 640.

South of the theatre, at the top of Jebel al-Ashrafiyeh, the Abu Darwish mosque is built in alternating layers of black and white stone.

The Abdullah Mosque, named after the first monarch of the Hashemite kingdom, is a sparkling, blue-domed modern structure west of the city centre, overlooking the national parliament. It is the city's one mosque open to non-Muslims.

Darat el-Funum

Artists from Jordan and other Arab countries exhibit their works in this pretty house on the Jebel Weibdeh, which also stages plays and concerts.

Rujm el-Malfouf

On the west side of town, adjoining the Department of Antiquities office, this ancient, massive, round stone tower is the best preserved of twenty believed to

20

have been built at the end of the Ammonite era (7th century BC). It was probably part of the defence system under Assyrian rule.

Kan Zaman

A short drive south of the capital, this restored Jordanian village dating back to the 1900s has been transformed into an attractive craft and restaurant complex. It offers a good representative collection of traditional Bedouin and other regional artwork. You can watch the glassblower and woodcarvers at work.

Wadi Kharrar (Bethany)

In the late 1990s, archaeologists excavated a site thought to be the place where Christ was baptised, in a marshy area between Tell el-Kharrar and the river Jordan, 40 km (25 miles) from Amman, north of the Dead Sea. The Vatican recognized the authenticity of the site of Bethany in 1999 and intends to build a huge church there. The ruins date from several periods, including the 1st century AD, and are now open to the public. It is estimated that at least 16 churches were built here; parts of the mosaic floors of the North Church and the John-Paul II Church can be admired. You can also see a 4th-century pilgrims' hostelry, and 5th-century Rhotorios monastery and monks' cells carved out of the rock.

The area was fed by an ingenious irrigation system carrying water to cisterns which are till visible. Some of the pools were used for baptism ceremonies and were big enough to hold 300 people. The excavations are still ongoing, and the site is attracting more and more visitors, a boon for the local economy.

Salt

The former provincial capital under Turkish rule, just 30 km (18 miles) northwest of Amman, Salt has remained largely intact from its late-19th and early-20th-century commercial golden age thanks to having been passed over as King Abdullah's Transjordanian capital in favour of Amman. The town is worth a visit for its handsome Ottoman houses of buff limestone with elegant bay windows and wrought-iron balconies. One of the finest houses, the Salt Zaman, is now a traditional Arabian café and craft shop decorated with Ottoman and Bedouin antiques from the owner's personal collection.

The town's craft school (open for visits) is renowned for its weavers, potters and silk painters.

Jerash (Gerasa)

This jewel among the Romans' Decapolis cities, some 50 km (30 miles) north of Amman at the edge of the Jordan Valley, has

survived astonishingly well, protected over the centuries by the desert sands. The Seleucid city was held by the Jewish Hasmonaean dynasty, principally Alexander Jannaeus (103–76 BC), until it was annexed and expanded by Pompey around 64 BC.

The bold sweep of its streets, colonnaded shops, theatres and temples justifiably place Jerash second only to Petra among Jordan's attractions. It is a place to be visited at a leisurely pace, to stroll around as you would any pleasant modern town.

Visit the acclaimed monuments but explore, too, the unsung charms of hidden corners and alleyways.

Hadrian's Arch

The first of the town's ancient monuments to be encountered by visitors arriving from Amman, this triple archway commemorates the visit of Emperor Hadrian in AD 129. Its opulent yet graceful style reflects the Roman emperor's taste for both Greek and Oriental culture. His visit ushered in a golden age for the city under his successors, Antoninus Pius and Marcus Aurelius. At the base of the columns flanking the three arches, notice the ornate acan-

Detail of the backdrop of Jerash's South Theatre.

thus-leaf calyx above each plinth, which seem to be more Egyptian than Greek.

Hippodrome

Only by its rounded oblong form is the ruin next to Hadrian's Arch recognizable as a stadium for chariot racing and other sports. Of uncertain date—best guess 3rd century AD—it seated some 15,000 spectators in its 16 rows of stone benches. Archaeologists believe that the stadium in part also housed pottery and stone-masons' workshops and that in the 7th century the Persians used it for polo.

South Gate

Built around the same date and in the same style as Hadrian's Arch, this is the entrance to ancient Gerasa proper. The Roman city wall into which it was integrated was replaced in Byzantine times by another one 3.5 km (2 miles) in circumference, doubling the diameter, but little of it remains today. Inside the gate on the left was a market area, with the remains of an olive press nearby.

Oval Forum

A colonnade of Ionic pillars embraces the graceful curve of this magnificent granite-paved plaza, which is for many the single most handsome monument in Jordan. It was the meeting place for vis-itors to the city using the South Gate, for citizens coming from the shops on the main thoroughfare to the north, and for pilgrims heading for the Temple of Zeus. Greek inscriptions on columns on the south side proclaim the names of wealthy citizens who paid for its construction. The major structures in ancient Gerasa were more often paid for by private sponsorship than from state funds. In the centre, rising from the remains of a podium that once supported a statue, is a column recently erected to bear a torch for the Jerash summer arts festival.

Temple of Zeus

West of the forum, within the old city walls, the shrine to the chief god in the Greek pantheon was built in 162 AD as part of the building boom that followed the visit of Emperor Hadrian. It stands on the site of an earlier temple to Zeus dating back to the 2nd century BC, which also served as a storage house for temple treasure from neighbouring Philadelphia during the Hasmonaean invasion from Judaea.

The vaulting of the lower substructure has been restored, but the columns of the temple on top give only an approximate idea of its former splendour. The upper level affords a fine view over the ancient city and modern Jerash to the east.

JERASH FESTIVAL

Queen Noor inaugurated the international arts festival of Jerash in summer 1981. Every July, theatre troupes, ballet and folkdance groups from all over the Middle East and Europe perform against the dramatic Roman backdrop of ancient Gerasa's South Theatre. The performances are accompanied by exhibitions of traditional craftwork—Bedouin carpets, jewellery, embroidery, glassware and ceramics.

South Theatre

Immediately beyond the temple, this beautifully restored edifice, now the centrepiece of Jerash's arts festival, is the larger of the town's two theatres. Inscriptions displayed outside the theatre on the east side attest that it was built under Emperor Domitian (AD 81–96), though his name has subsequently been obliterated because of the tyrant's evil reputation. Other names inscribed inside the theatre honour private sponsors who financed blocks of seats in the auditorium for over 3,000 spectators. Notice the Greek lettering on the rows for reserved seating closer to the front.

The exceptional acoustics of the theatre enable you to hear the proverbial pin drop from the uppermost rows, with the extra advantage of a great view over the town. At the rear of the stage, the finely carved stone equivalent of the modern backdrop originally had an upper storey over the stage-entrance arches and niches for statues.

Besides drama and musical performances, the theatre was used for oratory contests and sports events.

Main Street

The town's splendid colonnaded *cardo,* the main north-south thoroughfare, extends 800 m (875 yd) from the Oval Forum to the North Gate. It is intersected on either side of the Temple of Artemis by two east-west cross streets *(decumanus).* The original Ionic columns of the *cardo* were embellished with Corinthian capitals when the street was widened during the town's reconstruction in the 2nd century AD. The colonnade was part of a roofed portico providing shade for pedestrians visiting the shops on either side of the street. On the left, a short way from the Oval Forum, four taller columns form the entrance to the food market *(macellum).* Chariot and wagon wheels have left ruts in the stone paving. You can also see gutters to a central drainage system complete with round stone access covers.

On the other side of the street from the *macellum,* a small museum has an interesting display of finds from the excavations—gold jewellery, glassware, lamps, coins and ceramic theatre tickets.

Crossroads

The bases of four pedestals in the middle of the *cardo* are all that remain of the Southern Tetrapylon, a four-columned structure built over the intersection with the South Decumanus. A pyramidal roof probably sheltered statues placed in niches between the columns.

To the right, the cross street runs downhill to a bridge spanning the Chrysorhoas river, leading to ancient Gerasa's residential district, now buried under modern Jerash.

Following the cross street in the opposite, westerly direction, you reach the excavated foundations of three Umayyad houses of the 8th century, probably representing a subdivision of one larger mansion built around 660.

Cathedral

The gateway to the "cathedral" of Gerasa's early Christians stands behind eight tall columns just north of the Southern Tetrapylon. It was built in the 4th century from elements of a temple to Dionysus. The gateway was the temple's propylaeum (vestibule), from which a staircase leads to the Shrine of St Mary, with traces of an inscription to Mary and the Archangel Gabriel. In keeping with the church's spiritual predecessor, the god of wine and mystic revelry, the miracle of Jesus turning water into wine was celebrated in the cathedral's Fountain Court.

Nymphaeum

Just north of the cathedral's gateway, two pairs of imposing columns form part of the town's main fountain (AD 191) dedicated to divine water nymphs. The monument's lower storey was originally clad in green marble, with an upper storey of orange and green painted plaster beneath a hemispheric dome. Sculptures of nymphs cavorting with dolphins decorated the façade, and water spouted into basins from seven lion's heads—all of which have since disappeared. The large red granite basin was added in the Byzantine era.

Propylaeum

A triple gateway, previously the grand entrance to the Temple of Artemis further west, was transformed by the Byzantine Christians in the 6th century into what became known as the Propylaeum Church. Beyond it is the temple's monumental staircase, part of the Processional Way that began at a bridge over the Chrysorhoas river.

Temple of Artemis

Gerasa's most venerated monument was dedicated to the town's patron divinity, Artemis, goddess of fertility and hunting. Ongoing excavations are still uncovering the colonnades that bordered the vast esplanade where the worshippers used to congregate while the priests officiated in the temple above. Laymen can now make their way to the temple's elevated podium on which a double row of columns with delicately carved Corinthian capitals form the rose-hued peristyle.

Byzantine Churches

Grouped around an atrium southwest of the Temple of Artemis are the remains of three out of fifteen Byzantine churches so far uncovered in ancient Gerasa. It is believed there are many more. The Church of Saints Cosmas and Damian ("the holy money-less ones", twin brothers martyred in the 4th century) isn't open to the public, but its mosaics of saints, birds and animals, dated 533 and considered the finest in Gerasa, are visible from a wall overlooking the site.

Mosaics found in the churches of St John (centre) and St George (to the south) were severely damaged in the 8th-century icono-clastic campaign waged by Christian zealots against images of Christ and the saints.

Synagogue Church

To the north of the church of Saints Cosmas and Damian are traces of a 2nd-century BC synagogue—mosaics depicting the Jewish menorah (the seven-branched candelabra), the *lullav* (palm branch), and the *shofar* (ram's horn) used to trumpet in the New Year and Day of Atonement. In the 6th century AD, a church was built over the site with a new geometric mosaic.

North Theatre

Rising between the Temple of Artemis and the North Decumanus is the smaller of the town's two theatres, seating some 1,600 spectators. It served as an open-air assembly hall for municipal government. Some of the seats bear the names of clans represented on the council. From here there's a pleasant view of the valley to the north of the city.

North Gate

The North Gate was artfully designed in a wedge shape, which enabled its two façades to stand perpendicular to the Cardo and the Roman road to Pella that meet each other at an acute angle. The gate's bastions are Byzantine. Notice the handsome diagonal paving of this northern section of the Cardo, still lined with Ionic colonnades as it was in the 1st century.

Entered by a wooden drawbridge, the Arab castle Qala'at ar-Rabadh commands the Jordan Valley and three wadis.

Ajlun

The drive to Ajlun's medieval castle 15 km (9 miles) west of Jerash abandons arid desert and takes you into the greenery of the Jordan Valley, through rolling hills clad with groves of pine and olive trees.

Qala'at ar-Rabadh

Perched on a hilltop, the fortress was built in 1184 by a relative of Saladin, Izz ad-Din Usama, as defence against the feuding local emirs (who unwittingly helped him build it), and to counter the Crusaders' Belvoir castle across the valley. The urgency was relieved just three years later by Saladin's momentous victory at Hattin, but Usama's successors expanded the fortifications, just in case. The original four-square castle was strengthened by the addition of bastions, a new gateway and a dry moat. It was partly destroyed by Mongol invaders in 1260 but reconstructed by their Mameluke conquerors under Sultan Al-Dhaher Baybars. The Ottoman Turks used it briefly as an administrative centre before abandoning it to the Arab family found there by Swiss traveller Johann Ludwig Burckhardt prior to his discovery of Petra in 1812.

The roof of the tower next to the present entrance provides a thrilling view of the whole fortress and far over the Jordan Valley. From here, you can appreciate the castle's value as part of the chain of Arab defences, which relied on an early-warning system of flaming beacons extending from Baghdad to Cairo. Medieval pigeon-post from fortress to fortress covered the distance in half a day, while modern airmail takes a week.

Pella

North of Ajlun, in a green, well-watered valley near the village of Tabaqat Fahl, this sprawling archaeological site is off the beaten track for most tourists but gives a good insight into one of the more important Decapolis towns, from its prehistoric origins and beyond Roman conquest to the early Ottoman period. After stagnating under the occupation of the Hasmonaean rulers of Palestine in the 1st century BC, it was captured by Pompey and redeveloped by the Romans.

The most visible remains are those of early Christian churches, the 5th-century Byzantine Great Basilica with monumental stairway, and a Mameluke mosque of the 13th and 14th centuries. The small odeon is the best preserved monument of the Roman city. There are also prehistoric tombs and other remains from the Bronze Age.

Umm Qais

The village is located at Jordan's northwestern tip at the site of the ancient city of Gadara. From its plateau above the Jordan Valley,

DECAPOLIS: THE BIG TEN

Founded in large part by Alexander the Great and his Seleucid and Ptolemaic successors around 323 BC, the ten cities of the Decapolis were, in their spacious layout and imposing monuments, models of urban planning for the whole Middle East. Their cosmopolitan character is attested by the frequent juxtaposition of Greco-Roman temples, Jewish synagogues and later Christian churches. Organized into a league under the Romans, the prosperous cities became a sort of NATO cum European Union, operating as a defence league and customs union. Besides Jordan's Philadelphia (Amman), Gerasa (Jerash), Pella and Gadara (modern Umm Qais), the league also included Damascus (Syria) and Scythopolis (Beth She'an, now in Israel), the only member situated west of the Jordan. Their lifeline was the 500-km-long (310-mile) Via Nova Traiana, the longest stretch of Roman road in the East.

you look northwest across the border over Israel's Sea of Galilee to the town of Tiberias and, to the northeast, over Syria's plunging Yarmuk river valley to the Golan Heights. The view can be enjoyed from the café terrace of the resthouse at the entrance to the archaeological site.

Like many of the other Decapolis towns, Gadara was originally founded by the Ptolemies and captured in turn by the Seleucids and Hasmonaean Jews before Pompey seized it for the Romans. In this case, Pompey personally oversaw its rebuilding, because one of his favourite freedmen lived here. In 30 BC Emperor Augustus gave the town to his ally King Herod of Judaea, which incensed the population. Its most prosperous era came after Trajan incorporated it into the Roman province of Arabia in AD 106.

Byzantine Basilica

Remains of the ancient Roman city can be seen mainly in recycled masonry incorporated into the 6th-century Byzantine basilica on a terrace below the resthouse. A colonnaded atrium of white Corinthian pillars makes an imposing approach to the church proper, taking the customary form of a square surrounding an octagon, bordered by contrasting pillars in black basalt.

GONE WITH THE SWINE

Gadara's name lives on in the New Testament story of the Gadarene swine, as related by Matthew, Mark and Luke. Jesus meets two madmen near Gadara and saves their souls by transferring the devils in them to a herd of 2,000 pigs, which promptly plunge to their death in the Sea of Galilee. To do so, they would have had to run for several kilometres to reach the sea, no small accomplishment for pigs.

Theatre and Ancient Gadara

South of the basilica is a theatre of black basalt, where the auditorium, reached through a vaulted tunnel, seated 3,000 spectators: Roman Gadara was famous for its performing arts. This was evidently a prosperous city, and its plan can be seen as a colonnaded main thoroughfare, the Decumanus Maximus, lined with sturdy barrel-vaulted shops, with cross-streets paved in black basalt. Other remains reveal monumental public baths, a hippodrome and triple gateway leading west to Galilee.

The 19th-century residence of an Ottoman merchant houses a museum set around a courtyard of pomegranate trees, exhibiting sarcophagi, sculpture, mosaics, glassware and ceramics.

► EASTERN DESERT
Qasr al-Hallabat, Qasr Azraq, Shaumari Wildlife Reserve, Qasr Amra, Qasr Kharaneh

Beyond Amman, to the east, the desert stretches in a broad band to the Iraqi border, with Syria to the north and Saudi Arabia to the south. The Romans built castles here as frontier posts for the eastern edge of their empire. In the 8th century, the Umayyad caliphs, the first Islamic dynasty after the death of Mohammed, took over some of the sites closer to the Jordan Valley to erect winter palaces, often no bigger than the desert equivalent of country houses. Some served as caravanserai—fortified inns for merchant caravans. The best-known, at Azraq, was a headquarters for Lawrence of Arabia and Faisal ibn Hussein on their way north to Damascus. Four of the most accessible "desert-castles", and the Shaumari Wildlife Reserve, can be visited on a one or two-day round trip from Amman.

Qasr al-Hallabat
This is the first stop on the desert circuit, heading north from Amman via Zarqa. The castle is in a sad state of repair but gives a good impression of its successive

Azraq oasis, a welcome change from the dun-coloured desert.

uses as a desert stronghold. The 2nd-century Roman fort, built during the reign of Caracalla, was probably transformed into an early Christian monastery before the Umayyads took it over and added a mosque, mosaic floors and mural paintings. Close by are the ruins of the fort's thermal baths, Hammam as-Sarah.

Qasr Azraq
The castle is 3 km (nearly 2 miles) north of the village settled by Druze refugees from Syria in 1920. It stands in one of the eastern desert's largest oases, the freshwater pools winning it the Arabic name of Azraq—"blue". After setting up his headquarters here at the end of 1917, Lawrence of Arabia wrote of "the blue fort on its rock above the rustling palms, with the fresh meadows and shining springs of water". The modern roads and village have tampered a bit with the idyllic image, but palm trees and pools are still there. And the fort's monumental door built of a single 3-ton basalt block still creaks ponderously on its hinges to admit the wayfarer to its medieval precincts. Indeed, much of the Roman masonry has been recycled, some bearing Latin ref-

erences to emperors Diocletian and Maximian. Just inside the entrance, a flight of stairs leads up to the wretchedly austere quarters where Lawrence shivered in the cold, damp winter.

Shaumari Wildlife Reserve

Set amid trees some 10 km (just over 6 miles) southeast of Azraq, the nature reserve has been set up to breed and protect the rare oryx antelope and onager (a variety of wild ass), along with gazelle, ostrich, hyena, jackal and wolf. The reserve covers 22 sq km (8.5 sq miles) of desert, scrub and oasis. Besides a small zoo, an observation platform gives vistors an occasional glimpse of the animals running wild. The oryx in particular had practically disappeared from its native Arabian peninsula until Jordanian conservationists embarked on this programme, while the onager was previously limited, in ever dwindling numbers, to Iran and Turkmenistan.

Qasr Amra

West of Azraq and just north of the Amman highway, these 8th-century baths and hunting lodge were a delightful piece of self-indulgence created for Caliph Walid I (705–15). After building the Great Umayyad Mosque of Damascus, the fervently orthodox Muslim took time out to relax in this highly ornate home-from-home. The baths, chambers and "throne room" are vividly decorated in predominant shades of reds, greens, browns and blues, with often erotic wall paintings, a rare event in Islamic art that subsequently forbade all figurative representation. The strong Hellenistic influence is clear in hunting scenes and allegorical themes from Greek mythology, particularly in the baths' domed *caldarium*, or hot room.

Walid died at the ripe old age of 40, having enjoyed a life devoted to pleasure.

Qasr Kharaneh

Built in the 8th century, this most handsome of the eastern desert Umayyad "castles" clearly served as a caravanserai. The compact but sturdy four-square limestone edifice has rounded towers at each corner and an imposing entrance in its southern wall leading to lofty camel stables and merchants' quarters surrounding the inner courtyard. The upper floor has several larger rooms, notable for their supporting roof-domes on a system of squinches and pendentives, one of the earliest instances of Islamic architecture drawing on this decorative Byzantine and Persian technique. Climb up to the roof terrace for the view it affords over the desert.

To any human being who takes a dip in it—swimming is almost impossible—the Dead Sea seems like a huge bowl of over-salted soup. In ancient times, it was also known as Salt Sea. Jordan shares

FIRE AND BRIMSTONE

The best evidence that the southern end of the Dead Sea is the probable location of Sodom and Gomorrah is the abundance of foul-smelling chemicals. This is what brimstone and fire smelled like when they destroyed the Bible's most notorious pits of sin. Scholars locate here the Genesis story of Abraham's nephew Lot fleeing with his family, when his wife took one last forbidden look back and was turned into a pillar of salt. Five Bronze Age settlements on the southeastern shore have been identified as likely candidates for the Bible's five cities in the Valley of Siddim, Bab ed-Dhra being the best bet for Sodom, and Numeira for Gomorrah. Any of a hundred natural "pillars" on the sea's salt flats, the area called Southern Ghor, may contain Mrs Lot's mortally curious soul.

with Israel this 76-km-long (48-mile) stretch of water, 17 km (10 miles) at its widest point, the lowest point on earth and one of the wonders of the Middle East. Hot desert air evaporates freshwater inflow from the Jordan river too fast for most living organisms to survive. So there are no fish, not even rollmops, but plenty of minerals: inexhaustible supplies of table salt, together with industrial potassium, bromide and magnesium, make up 30 per cent of the water. They are exploited industrially at the southern end of the sea around "Potash City".

Dead Sea Beaches

The north shore beaches with cabins and showers are located 55 km (34 miles) southwest of Amman, near the village of Suweima. A resthouse has a restaurant on a terrace directly overlooking the sea, and there are also comfortable resort establishments offering massage treatment, mud baths and natural hot water springs. It was in the Dead Sea Spa Hotel that Jordanian and Israeli diplomats worked out the details of their peace treaty in 1994. Wherever you bathe, be sure to make abundant use of the showers—shampoo three or four 33 times to cleanse your hair of the salt that is said, like the local mud, to be excellent for skin ailments. If you are on the seashore at sunset, there is a lovely distant view of slender minarets in Jerusalem on the western horizon.

King's Highway

On a mountain ridge east of the Dead Sea, the picturesque route between Amman and Petra has had its royal name at least since biblical times. The Israelites, on their way north before crossing into Canaan, asked the Amorite ruler to let them pass along this route, promising not to disturb his farmland, vineyards or wells. The Nabataeans used it as their main trade road for goods from Arabia, and Emperor Trajan reconstructed it for his troops and merchants as part of the Via Nova Traiana. Christian pilgrims used it in Byzantine times to visit monasteries, churches and other holy places around Madaba and Moses' Mount Nebo, and later Muslims followed it on their way to Mecca. Crusaders built castles along it to protect their eastern flank.

Madaba

Some 30 km (nearly 20 miles) southwest of Amman, the town now celebrated for its Byzantine mosaics appears in the Bible as Medeba. It was allotted to the Hebrew tribe of Reuben before being conquered by the Moabites and passing into the hands of the Nabataeans and Romans. Thereafter it was developed by Byzantine Christian emperors as a major place of pilgrimage. Today, half the town's population is Christian, most of them Greek Orthodox.

"Church of the Map"

Most famous of all Madaba's mosaics is the 6th-century map of the holy places in the biblical world. Now housed in the 19th-century Church of St George, it was originally found amid the ruins of a church built in the reign of Emperor Justinian (527–65). Although in a fragmentary state, it still gives a fascinating glimpse of how the earliest Christian pilgrims saw their Holy Land destinations, labelled in Greek. Originally a rectangle 25 m (82 ft) long, it covered the area from Tyre and Sidon in Lebanon down to Egypt, between the Mediterranean coast and the eastern reaches of Jordan. But like the church, the map is oriented to the east, rather than the north, as follows: the top looks east towards Karak fortress; the right depicts the south as far as the Nile Delta; the bottom takes in the west to Ashdod and Ashkelon on the Mediterranean; to the left is the north, with the Jordan river and Jericho. In the middle of the fragment is the Dead Sea with two boats; their crew or passengers have been obliterated at some point by iconoclasts. Below the sea is Jerusalem, where you can make out the Church of the Holy Sepulchre, the Citadel and the Damascus and Jaffa Gates.

Madaba Archaeological Park

A group of handsome Ottoman houses on Prince Hassan Street leads to a collection of mosaics from archaeological excavations in the region. Inside the park's entrance on Abu Bakr Street is Jordan's oldest mosaic, recovered from King Herod's palace at nearby Mukawir (ancient Machaerus), where Salome danced for John the Baptist's head.

The Hippolytus Hall mosaics, depicting the legend of Phaedra's passion for her stepson, Hippolytus, comes from a Madaba house of the 6th century AD, found beneath the Church of the Virgin which was in turn discovered under the floor of a later house in 1887. Of the church's own fragmentary mosaic, only a geometric pattern and religious inscription survive. Other mosaics have been recovered from the Acropolis Church at Ma'in.

Museum

The exhibits in the museum, near the Church of the Apostles, enable you to compare Roman mosaics, notably a procession of Bacchus and his revellers, with religious themes of Byzantine mosaics executed in fundamentally the same style. Other dis-

---

THE ART OF MOSAICS

If the Romans were the most prolific exponents of mosaic design in temples, houses, shops and public baths, their Byzantine successors carried it to its highest level of artistic expression in their churches. Floors or walls were inlaid with coloured squares of marble or other stone as well as glass, clay or wood. The artists depicted scenes from Greek and Roman mythology, biblical stories and scenes of everyday life—hunting, fishing, farming and household work. Many figures were chiselled out of the mosaics by iconoclasts, either 8th-century Byzantine Christians, or Muslims and Jews, all opposed to the potential idolatry of depicting human beings or animals. In some cases, the offending creatures were replaced by a plant or geometric pattern. In Madaba's mosaic removed from the Ma'in Acropolis Church, a tree covers all the traces of an ox except for its hooves and tail.

plays include bronzes, ceramics and glassware from the region's archaeological finds, as well as traditional folk costumes.

Mount Nebo

Just northwest of Madaba, the mountain on which Moses had his first and last view of the Promised Land has two peaks, El-Mukhayyat and Siyagha. Most scholars have still not decided which of them is more likely to have been his vantage point. In the valley around Mukhayyat are several churches and monasteries from the 5th and 6th centuries, but early Christians plumped for the more northerly Siyagha peak on which to build the Moses Memorial Church. Certainly the view here would have warmed the cockles of the prophet's heart—reaching far out over the Dead Sea and, on the proverbial clear day, all the way to what are now Bethlehem, Jerusalem, the green oasis of Jericho and Ramallah. As the book of Deuteronomy tells it, Moses died on Mount Nebo aged 120 and was buried somewhere in the valley, "but no man knows his grave to this day". That was true when it was written, probably in the 7th century BC, and is still true today.

In the region of Karak, the land is cultivated in terraces.

In the church itself, much reworked over the centuries and excavated since 1933 by Franciscan monks, remains of an original limestone structure dating back to the 4th century are now sheltered under a corrugated iron roof and adorned with modern stained-glass windows. To the left of the entrance is an older baptistery, lower than the rest of the church, whose floor is decorated with a fine 6th-century mosaic depicting vivid scenes of men fighting off lion, bear and wild boar, sheep grazing, and herdsmen leading an ostrich, a zebra and a camel.

Karak

At the southern end of the Dead Sea, the Crusaders' formidable 12th-century castle straddles the mountain ridge west of the King's Highway. The ramparts crown a steep glacis escarpment built against the mountainside, giving the medieval artillery unimpeded range over the valley. This is the slope down which the brutal Renaud de Châtillon hurled his prisoners. The castle makes use of ancient masonry from a Nabataean fortress. Still visible are the dungeons, knights' quarters and a kitchen with olive press. Remains of the Mameluke palace added in the 14th century include a castle keep. Its roof offers a magnificent view over the deserts of Israel and Jordan. 37

The ancient royal city of Petra carved out of the desert by the Nabataean merchants is the undisputed highlight of any visit to Jordan. Within easy reach are the medieval fortress of Shobak, the scenic splendours of the Dana nature reserve, the fabled Wadi Rum desert and the relaxing Red Sea resort town of Aqaba.

Petra

This is the stuff that the dreams of A Thousand and One Arabian nights are made of. A thrilling adventure awaits every visitor making his way along the Wadi Musa valley to the great Siq chasm, beyond which lie the treasures of the Nabataeans' stronghold. The town was given the name Petra by the Greeks, from *petros*, or "rock". It is easy to see why. The merchant princes hewed their monumental tombs, palaces, temples and treasury from the desert rock's sandstone in its natural hues of rose, gold and ochre. The architectural and sculptural styles draw on all the elegant Greek and opulent Oriental traditions encountered by these pre-Islamic Arabs on their travels throughout the Middle East and Mediterranean.

In this royal capital sprawling across a considerable area of mountain and desert valley, even a brief tour of the principal attractions—the treasury, theatre and monastery, the ingenious water-supply system and remains of the ancient city centre—will take a full day. To do them proper justice involves a more leisurely visit of two or even three days. For excursions to outlying monuments, like the shrine on Mount Haroun, and the sheer pleasure of taking in the wonders of the desert, many visitors are happy to stay a week.

Bab al-Siq

Literally "the Gateway of the Chasm", the broad path leading up to the entrance passage of ancient Petra starts out from the Visitors' Centre and follows the bed of the Wadi Musa (Moses River), totally dry for most of the year. The river takes its name from the biblical episode when Moses, faced with irate Israelites crying out in thirst, struck the rock twice with his rod, whereupon the water gushed out.

On the way to the Siq, you pass on either side what look like massive rectangular podiums, known

Glowing in the sun, the ornate façade of Petra's Treasury.

to the local Bedouin as Djinn (genie) blocks invested with mystical spirits, and thought to be Nabataean funerary monuments.

On the south side of the path are two monumental tombs of the 1st century BC: the Obelisk Tomb with four obelisks carved in the façade, and below it the Bab al-Siq Triclinium, a chamber containing benches on three sides for mourners attending the funeral banquet. Archaeologists have excavated more than 800 tombs and funerary banquet-halls of this kind in Petra.

The Siq

The main entrance to the Siq was once spanned by a monumental arch. The narrow corridor leading to Petra meanders through a natural cleft in the mountain's sandstone, occasionally narrowing to just 2 m (6.5 ft) wide, with the rockface towering high on either side. Notice the channels cut in the rock to direct floodwaters of the Wadi Musa to a dam (now replaced by a modern dam just before the entrance to the Siq). The water was diverted around the mountain to the city of Petra to keep the Siq chasm dry for year-round access.

Some of the road's original paving is still in place. Cut in the rock walls at various heights are sacred niches, sculptures and blocks for deities, some with dis-

GETTING AROUND

Here more than anywhere else in Jordan, you will need your best walking shoes. If you want to preserve your energy for the hikes inside Petra itself, there are horses or pony-traps to take you along the Wadi Musa valley as far as the entrance to the famous Siq gorge, leading to the ancient site. Even these forms of transport are restricted by the pressures of tourist traffic at high season. However you go, take it easy and carry some mineral water with you. Vendors sell it along the way, but at an understandably higher price than away from the site.

cernible Greek inscriptions. Most magical of all is the subtle play of light and shadow, sometimes a single sun-beam cutting through the dark to illuminate the ancient sculptor's work. At its narrowest, the path takes one last bend and the view imposes on every newcomer an involuntary halt, especially when the daily brief but brilliant shaft of daylight illuminates the scene: ahead is El Khazneh, Petra's magical grand treasury.

El Khazneh

Carved from the rose-hued rock face opposite the exit of the Siq is the most beautiful and celebrated of Petra's monuments, probably fashioned in the 1st century BC. Film fans will recognize it from the final sequence of *Indiana Jones and the Last Crusade*. The majestic symmetrical two-storey façade is a subtle combination of Corinthian-style columns embracing niches and deeper recesses for statues. They frame an elegant central *tholos*—a cylindrical domed structure—over the monument's entrance.

In keeping with the eclectic style of Nabataean architecture, the sacred figures and symbols originally gracing the monument covered a broad spectrum of the Mediterranean pantheon: the Egyptian fertility goddess Isis, the Greeks' divine twins Castor and Pollux, and the Nabataeans' principal god, Dushara, who was the nomadic merchants' version of the Syrians' Hadad and the Greeks' Zeus.

The stone urn crowning the *tholos* was long thought to conceal golden coins and jewels, and local Bedouin tried to break it open with rifle shots. This explains the urn's "battle-scarred" condition and why the monument is traditionally known as the Treasury—indeed more fully the Pharaoh's Treasury, because all fabled riches hereabouts were attributed to Egypt's pharaohs. Most modern scholars agree that the "treasury" is in fact a monumental tomb, with perhaps the functions of a temple comparable to the great funerary temples in Egypt's Valley of the Kings. It is unlikely to have been a pilgrimage temple because of the limited access through the Siq.

The simple interior is in sober contrast to the effusive baroque façade. An upper main chamber was perhaps the burial place for the deceased, while side-chambers served the family or priests officiating at funerary rituals.

Theatre

Beyond El Khazneh, the Wadi Musa winds past several tombs to the Nabataeans' Roman-style theatre. Like the treasury, this was almost entirely hewn from the mountain rock. Created in the 1st century AD, it provided 45 rows of seats for several thousand spectators.

Royal Tombs

Royal perhaps only in scale and their splendid colouring in the natural hues of the rock, a series of elaborately carved tombs are set in the cliffs across the Wadi Musa east of the theatre. From south to north: the grandiose Urn Tomb, so named for the urn above the pediment, was consecrated, according to its Greek inscription, as a Byzantine church in the 5th century under Bishop 41

Jason; the Silk Tomb, smaller and weather-damaged, is notable for its brilliant striated colours; the Corinthian Tomb, also heavily eroded, recalls the ornate façade of El Khazneh; the Palace Tomb, the largest here, seems to imitate the style of a Roman palace and may be the city's youngest construction.

Ancient City Centre

Petra is not just a necropolis. Archaeologists are uncovering more and more remains of the prosperous royal capital that lay further down the Wadi Musa. Of both Nabataean and Roman construction, marketplaces, public baths, temples and a monumental ornamental fountain were built in the multicoloured local sandstone. They surround a long, once colonnaded main street that was constructed beside the course of the Wadi Musa.

Two major shrines stand at the western end of the street. Excavated since 1975, the Temple of the Winged Lions (1st century AD) was possibly dedicated to the Syrian goddess Atargatis or al-Uzza, counterpart to the Greeks' Aphrodite and symbolized by the lion. The vast temple known locally as Qasr al-Bint al-Faroun, "Palace of the Pharaoh's Daughter" (1st century BC), was perhaps dedicated to the Nabataean's chief deity Dushara, with a formidable altar for sacrifices of animals and frankincense.

Petra Museum

The museum containing Petra's archaeological finds is near the Forum Restaurant on the northwest outskirts of the ancient city centre. Among the sculptures, jewellery, ceramics and coins are statues of Dionysus and Aphrodite, the latter found in the theatre, and one of the winged lions from the temple.

El Deir

From behind the terrace of the Forum Restaurant, the uphill walk to El Deir—Arabic for "the monastery"—not too taxing if you take your time, is an exhilarating pleasure in itself. Donkeys are available for the foot-weary. You will pass several monumental tombs on the path, overlooking plunging ravines and pretty river valleys festooned with wild flowers in spring. The Lion Triclinium is set back in a side *wadi* to the left of the path, with stone lions guarding the entrance to the funerary banquet hall and Medusa heads at either end of the frieze on the pediment. Pause frequently, not just to catch your breath on the stairway cut in the rock, but to look back at the magnificent views of the cliffs beyond the Wadi Musa below and the impressive royal tombs.

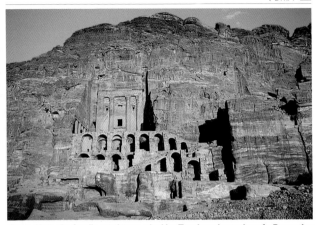

Carved into the fragile sandstone, the Urn Tomb and remains of a Byzantine church.

The final approach descends from behind El Deir, so that you do not see the imposing façade until you walk across an esplanade to the welcome shade of a café set in the rocks. The monument owes its designation as a monastery to Christian crosses inscribed in its inner walls, but in all likelihood it was originally a shrine dedicated to a Nabataean king of the 1st century BC. Larger than the treasury but similar in design (if less refined in its detail), the two-storey façade of El Deir is 45 m (nearly 150 ft) high and 49 m (160 ft) wide.

The esplanade, with remains of a stone altar in its northeast corner, is believed to have gathered worshippers for offerings and animal sacrifices. There is a superb view here over the El Ghor valley and across to Mount Haroun.

Behind the cavern sheltering the café, make your way out to the rocky promontories to the right and left, each affording grandiose panoramas of mountains and the distant desert.

High Place

On the way to the theatre from El Khazneh, an occasionally steep stairway off to the left takes you on a 30-minute climb to this imposing sanctuary for ritual

43

sacrifices, one of dozens around Petra. As you approach the High Place, notice on the left two obelisks thought to have been dedicated to Atargatis/Aphrodite. Up on the plateau is a rock-cut sunken court with stone benches along the sides, an oblong platform elevated in the centre for the offerings and steps leading to the altar. Beside the altar are basins and channels for draining off not blood, the scholars tell us, but water. If, as is generally believed,

SWISS SERENDIPITY

As is common with the world's great discoveries, intrepid Swiss traveller Johann Ludwig Burckhardt (1784–1817), came across Petra by happy accident and used the same "method" to stumble upon another marvel a few months later.

After university studies in England, the Lausanne-born son of an army colonel was hired in 1809 by a London-based association for promoting African discovery. He was to explore the caravan routes of the Sahara with a view to finding the source of the Niger river. It was not an easy job. The association sent him to Syria to steep himself in Arabic and Islam and then pass himself off as a Muslim, one Ibrahim ibn Abdallah. To travel through the Sahara, he was to link up with a caravan of pilgrims returning from Mecca. On his way down the Jordan Valley from Syria, he stopped off at the fortress of Karak, whose hill was known as Petra Deserti ("Rock of the Desert"), leading people to believe it was the site of the ancient Nabataean city. Burckhardt learned that the fabled royal capital was, in fact, hidden away in nearby mountains. As Ibrahim ibn Abdallah, the explorer persuaded his guide he wanted to pray at the shrine of Aaron on Mount Hor, and was led through the Siq chasm, becoming the first Westerner since the Crusaders 600 years earlier to behold El Khazneh and other wonders of Petra.

That was August 22, 1812. Seven months later, having made his way up the Nile from Cairo, Burckhardt came across some colossal pharaonic heads sticking out of the drifting sands of Nubia. He travelled on to Mecca without knowing that beneath the sands lay the colossal statues of the Abu Simbel shrine to Ramses II. Four years later he died of dysentery, never having got around to doing what he had actually been paid for. He had left his mark on posterity, however, by discovering Petra and by being the first Christian to penetrate the holy places of Islam, Mecca and Medina.

this plateau was used for Nabataean funerals, the platform may have served to expose the body of the deceased in the Persian Zoroastrian tradition, to be devoured by birds of prey—as on the Parsis' Towers of Silence in Bombay—and the water used to cleanse the precincts.

Instead of returning the way you came, you can continue on the path, which descends to the ancient city centre past a huge sculpted lion and an elaborate complex composed of the magnificent tomb of a Roman soldier, a colonnaded courtyard and a triclinium.

Aaron's Shrine

Southwest of the ancient city-centre, a path signposted to Aaron's Tomb takes pilgrims on a day's excursion to the top of Jebel Haroun (it's best to go with a guide). The mountain is identified by local belief with the biblical Mount Hor. Moses was said to have led his brother here, passing on the dying man's garments to his son Eleazar. Like Moses, Aaron died without setting foot in Israel, but would have had a view here of the Promised Land far away to the west. As a high priest, he is a much-revered figure in Islam, and the small white domed mosque built at the summit in the 14th century is said to shelter his tomb.

Beidha

About 8 km (5 miles) north of the visitors' centre is the prehistoric village sometimes known as "little Petra" because of its narrow gorge with similarly multi-coloured rockfaces separating it from the outside world. Beyond the chasm are remains of a settlement whose excavated tools, utensils and traces of cultivated wheat and barley have been carbon-dated at 7200 BC, making it one of the oldest agricultural communities in the Middle East. Other evidence suggests it was destroyed by fire 600 years later and was rebuilt with rectangular dwellings alongside the original part-subterranean round ones with stone walls and an inner core of wooden piles supporting a roof of clay and wattles. Outlines of these structures are still visible, and to the east what was possibly a sacrificial shrine of stone slabs and adjacent basins.

Shobak

Often visited by travellers on their way south from Amman, this castle can also make an easy day trip north of Petra on the way to the Dana nature reserve. Originally named Montréal, Shobak's castle was the first of the Crusaders' strongholds built east of the Jordan by King Baudouin in 1115 and among the last to hold out after Saladin's victories in Pales-

tine. Apart from remains of the Crusaders' church and chapel, most of what is visible now was added by Arab, Mameluke and Ottoman conquerors—a crenellated tower, dungeons, bath house and a reception hall.

Dana

The village of Dana, 60 km (37.5 miles) north of Petra, overlooks the nature reserve now occupying the slopes and dry riverbed of Wadi Dana. A couple of hundred Bedouin have settled down in attractively restored Ottoman limestone houses to practise their age-old handicrafts in jewellery, weaving and ceramics. They also tend the surrounding orchards that form the first layer of Dana's remarkably varied ecosystem. Starting at an altitude of 1,500 m (nearly 5,000 ft), the nature reserve descends from a Mediterranean landscape of cypress, citrus and olive groves, through sparse patches of pasture for sheep, goats and camels tended by other, semi-nomadic Bedouin, to a sub-tropical terrain supporting clumps of acacia, down to the more familiar sand-dune desert 100 m (over 300 ft) below sea level, and remains of the ancient copper-mining town of Feinan.

Sculpted by the winds, the fantastic forms of Wadi Rum.

The reserve offers good camping facilities, and nature-lovers can take an easy-going ramble through the whole system—three hours to the bottom. Day-trippers get at least a glimpse of the charms of a longer stay. On the way are opportunities to see some hundreds of species of plants, many of them unique to Dana. Among the reserve's nearly 200 species of birds, almost a record for a non-wetland area, are spotted and imperial eagles, kestrel, Cyprus warbler and Tristram's serin, a very rare yellow-and-brown finch. Mammals include the wild sand cat and the grey and white hoary Blanford's fox.

Copper-smelting at Feinan dates back to 4000 BC and continued through Roman and Byzantine times, leaving vestiges of a water-mill, aqueduct, cemeteries and early Christian churches.

Wadi Rum

Some two hours' drive south of Petra, the desert landscapes of Rum enchanted the great British adventurer-warrior-spy Lawrence of Arabia when he traversed them in his skirmishes with the Ottomans. (The film *Lawrence of Arabia* faithfully recorded its majesty.) Even the most blasé modern traveller will be bewitched by the startling colours and rock formations carved more artfully by the erosions of wind 47 and time than any Nabataean sculptor imagined possible. The towers of rock, sandy plateaux and chasms spanned by the odd natural rock-bridge offer great opportunities for the rambler, trekker or audacious climber, but also, for the more contemplative character, wonderful moments of tranquil meditation. Lawrence, of course, was an adept of both.

A resthouse at the unprepossessing modern village of Rum provides meals and overnight

EMIR DYNAMITE LAWRENCE

The adventurer's myth was carefully crafted by Lawrence of Arabia himself in his celebrated memoir, *The Seven Pillars of Wisdom*, first published in 1922. Besides describing his own role in leading the Arabs' guerrilla warfare against the Turks in World War I and the disparate sheikhs and army commanders he encountered, it also expounds his psychological, spiritual and profoundly mystical feelings in the desert. Born in Wales in 1888, Thomas Edward (who himself preferred just the initials T.E.) studied medieval history at Oxford, with a special emphasis on the military architecture of the Crusaders' castles. At the beginning of 1914, he combined archaeological excavations in the Middle East with map-making reconnaissance from Gaza to Aqaba to provide material both for Oxford University and the British Army. In 1916, he saw that Arab nationalism under Hussein ibn Ali, Emir of Mecca, and his sons Abdullah and Faisal, could help the British cause by undermining Germany's Turkish ally. Adopting Bedouin dress at the suggestion of an Arab friend, he led raids on the Turks' strategic bridges, trains and arms depots all along the Damascus to Medina railway. It was for these exploits that the Bedouin called him "Emir Dynamite". The key victory for Lawrence and the Arab guerrilla forces was at the vital garrison port of Aqaba, captured from the Turks on July 6, 1917 by surprise attack from the north after a two-month march through the desert. Lawrence claimed to have been captured and tortured by the Turks at Deraa but most historians doubt that it happened. He took part in the victory march into Damascus in October 1918.

Disillusioned by duplicitous Anglo-French diplomacy that ignored Arab national aspirations, Lawrence courteously but firmly refused his service decorations at a royal audience, leaving George V, as the king himself put it, "holding the box in my hand". Lawrence died in a motorbike accident in Dorset, England, in 1935.

accommodation in large communal Bedouin tents, with decent shower amenities. Other, simpler camping facilities are available just south of Rum at Abu Aina. It is certainly worth spending the night at one or the other to enjoy the beauties of both sunset and dawn in the desert.

Sights include the principal mountain Jebel Rum, 1,754 m (5,755 ft), with its Nabataean temple hewn from the rock on its eastern slope a short walk from the resthouse. Also in the rock face hereabouts are graffiti of camels, hunters and warriors carved by Thamudic nomads from Arabia in the 2nd or 3rd century AD. A little further away is the Ain ash-Shallaleh desert-spring, popularly known for no historical reason as Lawrence's Well.

Aqaba

At the northern tip of the Gulf of Aqaba, Jordan's only seaport has been coveted throughout its history as a gateway for Red Sea trade and Muslim pilgrimages to Mecca. Today, against its dramatic mountain backdrop, it is growing steadily as a beach resort. It has excellent facilities for diving, snorkelling, sailing, windsurfing and other water sports.

Spring, autumn and winters here are delightfully mellow, but the summer heat, starting already in May, can be oppressive.

Ups and Downs

Taking its modern name from Aqabat Aila, "the pass of Aila" on the way north to the Bedouin oasis of Ma'an (now southern Jordan's main trade centre), the town prospered as a port in this desert region thanks to its abundant coastal freshwater springs. Still being excavated on the Jordanian-Israeli border, the settlement of Tell al-Kaleifeh was once identified with King Solomon's Red Sea port of Ezion Geber but is now believed to be a later Edomite town of the 8th century BC.

Its strategic position made Aqaba the prey of Babylonians, Persians and Nabataeans. After AD 106, the Romans established it as the southern terminus of the Via Nova Traiana trade route from Syria. All that remains from the Byzantine era is some masonry recycled from old churches, and the medieval Islamic town is undergoing excavation.

The Crusaders came in 1116 and were upset to discover that the Red Sea was blue. Their castle was conquered by Saladin and later rebuilt by the Mamelukes.

After the Suez Canal and the Damascus to Medina railway deprived it of its Mecca pilgrim trade, Aqaba faded from history except for its moment of glory as the victorious battleground that spearheaded the Arab Revolt against the Turks in 1917.

The Fort

On the seaward side of the city centre, the Mamelukes' 16th-century fortress was built on the ruins of the Crusaders' castle which Renaud de Châtillon had used as a base for his pirate raids on Mecca pilgrims. Under Islamic rule, it served as a caravanserai, a fortified inn for the pilgrims and Red Sea traders. Besides the sturdy rounded towers and dungeons, you can still see remains of the camel stables and a small mosque. Notice the beams fashioned from palm-tree trunks. Prominent above the main entrance is the coat of arms of the Hashemite dynasty.

Museum of Aqaba Antiquities

In front of the fort, the museum of Aqaba's history shares its premises with the tourist office, part of which was in 1917 the handsome residence of Sheikh Hussein ibn Ali, Sherif of Mecca and great-grandfather of Jordan's King Hussein. The widespread trade that came through Aqaba can be seen in the collection of carved coral, glazed and painted pottery and coins from Ethiopia, Iraq, Egypt and China. Also here is the first milestone of the Romans' Via Nova Traiana.

Aquarium

The underwater marvels of the Red Sea and other seas are attractively displayed in a coral décor at the Aqaba Marine Science Station, about 9 km (nearly 6 miles) beyond the ferry port. Among the "stars" are tiger and hammerhead shark, sea turtles, clownfish, parrotfish, stingray and a host of smaller exotically coloured and camouflaged creatures. Ideal for those without time to go diving and see them for themselves.

Beaches

Most of the best-kept beaches are attached to the major hotels, but there is a good and less crowded beach at the National Tourist Camp a few kilometres south of the ferry port. The coral reefs here, pink but also jet black, are lovingly preserved—King Hussein was himself a keen diver. For a closer look at the coral, exotic fish and sea grasses, diving equipment is available at some of the big hotels, the Red Sea Diving Centre or the Royal Diving Centre 18 km (11 miles) south of town. Glass-bottom boats are a pleasant, if lazier, alternative.

Ayla

The remains of medieval Aqaba, founded in 650, can be seen opposite the Aqaba Gulf Hotel.

Aqaba's seafront is fringed by date palms.

Cultural Notes

Bedouin

Since the 1950s, when Jordan limited lands available for goat-grazing, many of the country's proud indigenous population have been obliged to abandon their time-honoured occupation as animal herders and settle down to traditionally despised agricultural work or, even worse, a job in town. The prestige of those able to stay on in the desert is classified according to the animals they tend. First and smallest in number are camel nomads, in a few large tribes covering vast areas of land; then come the sheep and goat nomads, a majority, and then the humble cattle nomads. Tribal life remains patriarchal, with the head of the family still known as the sheikh. Bedouin music originates with the solemn rhythmic declamation of poems from pre-Islamic times. Poet-musicians, often women, were revered for their supernatural powers; their satirical songs were used as weapons against tribal enemies.

Caravanserai

More than just an inn or hostelry, the "caravan-palace" where Arab merchants stopped to eat, sleep and water their camels, mules and horses was a veritable fortified hamlet. A few survive in the eastern desert, on the trade routes to Syria, Iraq and Saudi Arabia. Inside the walls were a mosque for prayer, sleeping accommodation, more or less spacious according to the status of master or servant, and courtyards where they met to exchange information, gossip and merchandise. As an ongoing investment in the merchants' custom, accommodation and services at the caravanserai were paid by the sultan for the first three days.

Islam

The name means in Arabic "submission to" Allah. Islam's sacred scripture, the Koran, covers all features of everyday life—marriage, property, work, eating, drinking and sleeping, as well as prayer. The Koran is Mohammed's presentation of Allah's message as he received it from the angel Gabriel. The Allah of the Koran is a loving, just and merciful god. His will determines the lives of all men and women. Their actions on earth determine their place in heaven or hell. The inspired merchant of Mecca (c.570–c.632) honoured the Jewish patriarchs and Jesus as pious but fallible prophets. As the last prophet, he had the last word.

Pillars of Faith

Five in number, these alone can earn salvation. Good Muslims recite each day: "There is no god but Allah, and Mohammed is his prophet". They pray five times a day facing Mecca and on Friday in the mosque, and when possible give alms to the poor and a gift to the mosque. During the month of Ramadan, Muslims should observe the fast and other laws of abstinence from sunrise to sunset. And at least once, unless they have the dispensation of poverty, they make the pilgrimage to Mecca—the *Hajj*.

Mosques

Their most prominent feature is the minaret, from the top of which the voice of the muezzin calls the faithful to prayer (these days the live call has generally been replaced by an amplified recording). The mosque is built around a courtyard with a fountain for ritual washing. The main prayer hall faces Mecca as indicated by the *mihrab*, a niche in the rear wall. Other features are a pulpit from which the Friday sermon is read and a platform for the *imam* leading prayers.

Nabataeans

From their capital at Petra, the Arabian merchants' many achievements included highly skilled technology in hydraulic engineering and metallurgy, and the development of a semi-cursive Aramaean script that formed the basis of modern Arabic writing. Their writing endures in rock-inscriptions, contracts and letters, but so far no literature as such has been found. The mixture of Assyrian, Babylonian and Hellenistic styles in their architecture and sculpture, as revealed at Petra and other Nabataean sites, reflects their extensive trading contacts across the Middle East.

The delicate, thin, red-painted pottery of their oil jars, perfume bottles and phials won favour throughout the Roman Empire and has been found as far away as Spain.

Circassians

A small minority of these Muslims from the northwestern region of the Caucasus settled in Jordan during mass migration following defeat by the Russians in 1864. They prospered as farmers and fruit-growers in the Jordan Valley and have maintained their Caucasian language and many of the pre-Islamic customs involving fertility rites and sacred groves of trees.

53

Shopping

The warm and friendly nature of Jordanian Arabs makes shopping here a pleasant experience. Whatever you're looking for, proceedings often begin with an offer of a cup of coffee or tea. This is a time-honored gesture of Arab hospitality and involves no obligation or pressure to make a purchase. Indeed, to decline the offer may hurt the shopkeeper's feelings. A couple of tips for anyone in the market for a relatively cumbersome gift like a Bedouin carpet or large piece of pottery and leaving Jordan from Amman or Aqaba: save your purchase till the end so you don't have to carry a burden on your excursions through the desert, and pack an extra collapsible bag in your luggage.

Where?

You will find the largest selection of goods in and around Amman. The Gold Suq near the old citadel, principally along King Faisal Street, is the best place to look for jewellery. Craftwork of Bedouin and Palestinian origin, the renewed production of which has been promoted by the energetic cultural activities of the Queen Noor Foundation, can be found at the Jordan Design and Trade Centre. Besides such long-established craftware shops as Bani Hamid (Jordan River Foundation) at the First Circle just off Rainbow Street, or Artisanat at the Second Circle, shopping and workshop complexes have been set up on the outskirts of the capital in the attractively restored Ottoman houses of Kan Zaman or, to the north, at Salt Zaman. Here, you can watch weavers, potters and glassblowers at work.

Aqaba has its own gold suq in the city centre and Petra's Liwan craftware shop at the Visitors' Centre is a branch of the Jordan Design and Trade Centre. Dead Sea health and cosmetics products are available both in Amman, notably at the airport, and at the Dead Sea Spa.

What?

Best buys are finely crafted gold and silver jewellery, traditional clothes re-styled for modern tastes, and Bedouin or Palestinian craftware.

Bedouin weaving in vibrant colours is difficult to resist.

Antiques

It is illegal to export antiquities of artistic or archaeological value, but other antiques from the 19th-century Ottoman era, such as carpets, samovars, ornaments, glassware, narghile hookah pipes, even old jewellery, are allowed. When in doubt, ask an official before purchasing. Around ancient Nabataean or Roman sites, ignore vendors of old coins or statuary; these are either fake or illegal.

Copper and Brassware

Hand-crafted trays, coffeepots, tea kettles and samovars make very handsome gifts, but check the soldered joints for leakage. Copper cooking utensils should be lined with tin.

Clothing

One of the country's more successful craftwork projects since the 1970s has been the subtle marriage of traditional patterns of Bedouin and Palestinian weaving, in the finest of Middle Eastern cottons and silks, with the modern flair of European design. The result is an elegant, distinctively Jordanian line of blouses, skirts, dresses, jackets, boleros and waistcoats, together with appealing shawls and handbags as accessories. Men might like the 55

Bedouins' long, flowing *galla-bieh* tunic or the dashing *keffiyeh* headdress, a square of chequered cotton folded into a triangle and held down by a cord—red and white favoured by Bedouins, black and white by Palestinians.

Dead Sea Cosmetics
The salts and other natural minerals of the Dead Sea make much-prized skin-products, cosmetics, bath salts and the ingredients for a mud facial or mud bath.

Glassware and Ceramics
The blue, green, turquoise or rose-coloured glassware for which the West Bank town of Hebron has long been famed is also manufactured by Palestinian refugees and sold at the Hebron Glass Factory, located in the village of Naur southwest of Amman, on the road to the Dead Sea. Another time-honoured Palestinian product is the highly decorative "Jerusalem pottery"—with geometric patterns or motifs of peacocks, exotic fish, pomegranates and bunches of grapes.

Jewellery
Among the Bedouin, silver has long been the preferred metal for jewellery, worked into necklaces, bracelets, amulets, rings, even perfume bottles. Pendants are decorated with Arabic calligraphy or hammered from old silver

coins. Traditional patterns may be used for modern forms of ornament. These and gold chains or settings for precious stones can be found in the Gold Suq in Amman or its smaller equivalent at Aqaba. You will also find less expensive, but attractive beadwork in semi-precious stones or even Petra's colourful polished pebbles.

Rugs and Embroidery
Colourful if not as sophisticated as Turkish or Iranian carpets, traditional rugs woven by Bedouin women make attractive wall-hangings or mats. Many of them, designed as Muslim prayer mats, are conveniently small for packing. The same weaving techniques and sturdy woollen fabric are used for cushion covers and saddlebags. More delicate embroidery is used for table linen, pillowcases and quilts.

Sand Bottles
From the multicoloured desert of Petra and Wadi Rum come the sands that local craftsmen artfully spoon into bottles and then fashion with long needles into the shapes of camels, palm trees and exotic birds. A resident of Petra, Mohammed Abdullah Othman, developed the technique as a child, finding his colours—20 different hues—in their natural state in the hills around his home.

Dining Out

Like most of the cooking in the eastern Mediterranean and other countries that formed part of the Ottoman Empire, Jordan's cuisine draws mainly on the savoury Turkish tradition, with a strong emphasis on olive oil, adding its own Bedouin dishes and others from its Egyptian and Lebanese neighbours.

To Start With...

The appetizers, or *mezzeh*, are varied and copious enough to make a meal in themselves. Many restaurants wait politely till you've finished them before taking your order for the main course. Served with the flat pita-bread known locally as *khoubz*, a typical *mezzeh* assortment may include *hummous* (chickpeas pureed with a little lemon and olive oil); *baba ghannoush* or *mutabal* (a smooth mixture of aubergine and *tahina* sesame paste); *tabouleh* salad of cracked wheat with chopped tomatoes, parsley, mint and lemon juice; *kubbeh maqliyeh*, fried meatballs with minced onion inside a crust of cracked wheat; *ful medames*, brown beans cooked with olive oil, cumin, garlic and lemon juice; and don't forget a simple dish of olives—*zaytoon*. If you prefer to start with soup *(shorba)*, it will likely be made with beans, chickpeas or red lentils.

Main Dishes

For a quick midday meal, wayside stalls sell two very satisfying main dishes masquerading as snacks—*falafel* is a kind of pita-bread sandwich of savoury balls of minced chickpeas, onions and parsley, served with a fresh salad topped with *tahina* sesame paste; *shawarma* is a pita-bread pocket filled with thinly sliced spit-roasted lamb, known in Turkey as *döner* and in Greece as *gyros*. The centrepiece of any Bedouin banquet is *mansaf*, lamb served on a bed of rice and pine-kernels with a tangy topping of yoghurt sauce. Try the *maqlouba*, stewed lamb or chicken with sliced aubergines and rice, or the familiar *shish kebab*, skewered cubes of grilled lamb (done with chicken, it's called *shish ta'uk*). For spit-roasted chicken, ask for *farouj*. Fish *(samak)* is rare except on the Red Sea at Aqaba and best ordered grilled. Muslims never eat pork, deemed unclean.

Desserts

It is in the sweet department that the Turks have left their strongest mark—*baklava*, layers of filo pastry laced with runny honey and chopped nuts; *kanafah*, finely shredded pastry, again stuffed with nuts and honey; *ma'amoul*, dates or nuts with rose syrup; *qataif*, a Ramadan speciality of cheese pancakes and sweet syrup; *ruzz bi laban*, creamy rice pudding; and *halva*, sesame paste. For something less rich, tend toward the Jordan Valley's fresh figs, apricots, grapes, bananas, apples and oranges.

Drinks

Tea, the national drink and mark of hospitality, is occasionally served with mint or sage. The best coffee is drunk in small cups, Turkish-style; the Bedouin add a touch of cardamom. Allow the grounds to settle before sipping. European beer is bottled locally, and the most nervous travellers can be reassured by the ready availability of mineral water. The local aniseed spirit, *araq*, resembles the Greek *ouzo*. These and stronger alcoholic drinks—especially whisky—are widely drunk by Jordanians, although imported liquor tends to be very expensive.

Pounding the beans for that tasty coffee.

Sports

For many people, getting around Jordan's deserts is sport enough. The main sports opportunities, to make a real change from sightseeing, are down at the Red Sea resort of Aqaba or, for "dry land" leisure activities, in Amman.

Water Sports

Jordan's tiny stretch of Red Sea coast at Aqaba is much coveted by scuba-divers and snorkellers —not least because the waters are less crowded (with people, not fish) than at the neighbouring resort of Eilat in Israel. Besides the thousands of fish on display, the main attraction is the Gulf's beautiful coral reef. If your hotel does not provide diver training and rental of equipment itself, including powerful underwater cameras, it can direct you to the town's Royal or Red Sea Diving Centres.

There are also plentiful opportunities for windsurfing, water-skiing and sailing, as well as deepsea fishing from the coast or on chartered boats.

When swimming, wear plastic shoes to protect the soles of your feet from the prickles of sea urchins, sharp coral, and the poisonous jab of stonefish, which lie half-buried in the sea bed. (If you are stung by a stonefish, see a doctor immediately.) Other hazards to watch out for are the black and white lionfish with a mane of poisonous spines all around their heads, and stinging jellyfish that occasionally swim in shoals close to the shore, in particular the Portuguese man-of-war.

Desert Trekking

Hiking and rock-climbing are best at the Dana Nature Reserve, Wadi Rum and around Petra itself. The Visitors Centre at Petra can provide information about overnight camel treks or balloon flights (season from March to November).

Tennis and Golf

In Amman, hotels can advise about access through the town's clubs to tennis courts and the golf course near the airport.

Horseback Riding

Your hotel may help you use the facilities of the Arabian Horse Club. Horse and camel races are held at the Royal Racing Club in spring and summer.

The Hard Facts

To plan your trip, here are some of the practical details you should know about Jordan:

Airports
International and charter flights fly into Amman's Queen Alia International Airport, 32 km (20 miles) from the city, or Aqaba. Both airports provide banking, car-hire and tourist information office services, in addition to duty-free shop, restaurant and snack bar facilities. Domestic flights often use Amman's Marka airport.

Climate
You'll enjoy the mildest weather in autumn and especially the spring, when wild flowers are in bloom. Summer is long, from May to early October, and intensely hot and dry, though evenings are cooler. Winter is an ideal time for Aqaba—mellow days and warm seawater. Winter temperatures in Amman average 8°C (46°F), in Aqaba 16°C (61°F). Summer temperatures in Amman average 25°C (77°F), in Aqaba 32°C (90°F).

Communications
Jordan is installing a modern telecommunication system for fax and phone, but only in Amman is there a reasonable number of telephone cabins in the street. Hotel phone and fax are relatively efficient but exorbitantly priced. For efficiency's sake, high-performance mobile phones are your best bet. To make an international call from Jordan dial 00 then the country code (1 for Canada and the US, 44 for UK), area code and local number. Jordan's international code is 962. The area code for Amman is 06, for Aqaba and Petra 03.

Crime
Jordan poses no problem for personal security and people are generally honest. Pickpockets—very often a fellow tourist—may be a problem at the airport or in crowded hotel lobbies. Without being paranoid, don't tempt them with an open handbag or a wallet in the hip pocket. Put valuables in the hotel safe.

Driving
Nearly all international car hire firms have their offices in Amman, but you may find better

rates with smaller local companies. Be sure you have a valid national licence or International Driving Permit. Rental age limit is over 21. To avoid unpleasant surprises, check on the exact extent of varying insurance coverages, personal, fire, collision, theft, etc. Driving inside Amman can be more trouble than it's worth, but the main country highways are well signposted, most often in English and Arabic. Drive on the right, overtake on the left and watch out for goats and sheep.

Electricity

Almost all appliances take plugs with two round pins—only occasionally British-style three-pin— for 220 volt, 50 Hz AC. Major hotels provide transformers and adapters for North American appliances.

Emergencies

Most problems can be handled at your hotel desk. Remember: consular help is there only for critical situations, lost passports or worse, not for lost cash or plane tickets. Emergency telephone numbers: police **192**; ambulance and fire brigade **193**.

Essentials

You won't need much formal wear, though in general Arab custom expects you to dress more conservatively than you might back home, especially if your visits include a mosque. Pack a sunhat and add a sweater for cool evenings, raincoat in the winter. Good walking shoes are vital, and easy-to-kick-off sandals or moccasins for the mosques, where women need a headscarf. Include insect repellent, sun-block and a pocket torch (flashlight) for Petra's monuments.

Formalities

Passports must be valid at least six months beyond the date of arrival in Jordan. A visa is obligatory for citizens of non-Muslim countries; it may be procured in advance from the Jordanian embassy or consulate of your country, or on arrival at the airport. Those over 18 years old may import, duty-free, 200 cigarettes, 25 cigars, or 200 g tobacco, and one litre of spirits. There is no limit on the amount of foreign currency, although it must be declared on arrival.

Health

No vaccinations are compulsory, but it's a good idea to have vaccinations for hepatitis, polio, tetanus and typhus. In fact, apart from minor stomach upsets from change of diet, the big health hazard in Jordan is the sun. Watch out for sunstroke, heat exhaustion and dehydration. Keep to the

61

shade, wear a hat, use a good sunscreen and drink plenty of water. To be on the safe side, stick to bottled mineral water and carry anti-diarrhoea pills. For emergencies, make sure your health insurance covers holiday illnesses, as Jordan's social security does not extend to foreign visitors. Doctors, dentists and hospital staff in Amman are well trained, many speaking good English or German. If you expect to need prescription medicines, take your own as you may not find the exact equivalent on the spot.

Language

English is firmly entrenched as the Jordanians' second language. However, except for hotels or other tourist establishments, do not expect to find anything but Arabic spoken outside the major tourist sites.

Media

Most European newspapers and European editions of American dailies are available, a day or so late, in major hotels. The *Jordan Times* is the main English-language daily newspaper, while the *Star* appears weekly. Many major hotels receive BBC World Service, Sky News or CNN television. BBC radio is accessible on short wave. Jordanian state radio and TV also have English- and French-language programmes.

Money

The national unit of currency is the Jordanian Dinar (JD), with 1,000 *fils* to the *dinar*. Coins range from 5 *fils* to 1 *dinar*; banknotes from ½ to 50 *dinars*. Jordanians also calculate in *piastres* (10 *fils* = 1 *piastre*).

In addition to the big hotels, many major shops and restaurants in Amman, Aqaba and Petra will accept credit cards. Smaller establishments request Jordanian currency. Traveller's cheques are best purchased in US dollars or pounds sterling.

Opening hours

The following times are a general guide, as opening times vary.

Banks 8.30 a.m.–12.30 p.m.; and some also 3.30–5.30 p.m. in tourist areas.

Some *shops* open nonstop 8 a.m.–8 p.m., others 9.30 a.m.–1.30 p.m. and 3.30–6 p.m. Apart from the Suq, many close on Friday. All tend to close earlier during Ramadan.

Post offices open Saturday to Thursday, 7 a.m.–7 p.m. in summer and to 5 p.m. in winter; Friday, 7 a.m.–1 p.m.

While Petra's *museums* are open every day, most museums in Amman and Aqaba close on Tuesday, and in Jerash and Karak on Friday. Exact times vary seasonally, so please check with the local tourist office.

Photography

Film for video or cameras is readily available in Jordan. Choose film speeds to suit the country's brilliant desert light. Some museums have restrictions on the use of flash. Avoid photographing Muslims at prayer. For other equally obvious reasons, avoid photographing areas involving military security—airports, naval bases and border crossings.

Public holidays

January 1	New Year's Day
March 22	Arab League Day
May 1	Labour Day
May 25	Independence Day
June 9	King Abdullah's accession to throne
June 10	Army Day
November 14	Birthday of late King Hussein

Movable feasts varying with Muslims' lunar calendar:

Ramadan	Fast during 9th month of lunar year
Eid Al-Fitr	4–5 days at end of Ramadan
Eid Al-Adha	Feast of Sacrifice at end of month of Hajj pilgrimage to Mecca
1st of Muharram	Muslim New Year
Eid Al-Isra' wa'l Mi'raj	Mohammed's Ascent to Heaven

Public Transport

The air-conditioned buses of the Jordan Express Tourist Transport (JETT) company start from the JETT bus station and link Amman with Petra and Aqaba. Private companies use the Abdali and Wahdat bus stations. All over the country, minibuses cover long and short distances. Jordan's one passenger train, a steam engine on the historic Hijaz railway, runs only once a week. Private yellow taxis serve the major hotels and can be hailed in the street. The meter tends to run only by day, so agree on the price before starting out for your destination. White "Service-Taxis" shared by several passengers follow set routes and usually start off when full.

Time

GMT +2, and GMT + 3 in summer (April to September).

Tipping

Service is included in hotel and restaurant bills, but you can always add a little extra. Tipping is never obligatory but appreciated.

Toilets

You'll do best to take advantage of facilities at hotels or tourist restaurants.

63

INDEX

Ajlun 27–28

Amman 15–21
  Abdullah Mosque 20
  Abu Darwish Mosque 20
  Archaeological Museum 17–19
  Citadel 16–17
  Folklore Museum 19
  Forum 19
  Gold Suq 19
  Hussein Mosque 20
  Nymphaeum 19
  Odeon 19
  Popular Traditions museum 19
  Roman theatre 19
  Rujm el-Malfouf 20
Aqaba 49–50, 59
Ayla 50
Azraq 31
Bedouin 52
Beidha 45
Bethany 21
Burckhardt, J.L. 12, 44
Camels 5
Circassians 53
Crusaders 10–11
Dana 47

Dead Sea 33–34
Decapolis 28
Gadara 29
Gerasa 21–26
Hussein 13, 17
Islam 52–53
Jerash 21–26
Kan Zaman 21
Karak 11, 37
King's Highway 34
Lawrence of Arabia 48
Madaba 34–37
Mosaics 35
Mount Nebo 37
Nabataeans 9, 53
Pella 28
Petra 39–45
Qala'at ar-Rabadh 27–28
Qasr al-Hallabat 31
Qasr Amra 32
Qasr Azraq 31–32
Qasr Kharaneh 32
Salt 21
Shaumari Wildlife Reserve 32
Shobak 45–47
Sodom and Gomorrah 33
Umm Qais 28–29
Wadi Kharrar 21
Wadi Rum 47–49

GENERAL EDITOR
Barbara Ender-Jones
STAFF EDITOR
Alice Taucher
LAYOUT
Luc Malherbe
PHOTO CREDITS
Harald Mielke, pp. 1, 2;
Claude Hervé-Bazin,
covers, pp. 6, 10, 22, 36, 38,
43, 46, 51
Christine Osborne Pictures,
pp. 14, 18, 20, 55, 58
Bernard Joliat, pp. 27, 30
MAPS
JPM Publications;
Elsner & Schichor

Copyright © 2005, 1998
by JPM Publications S.A.
12, avenue William-Fraisse,
1006 Lausanne, Switzerland
E-mail:
information@jpmguides.com
Web site:
http://www.jpmguides.com/

Printed in Switzerland
Weber/Bienne (CTP) — 05/06/01
Edition 2005–2006

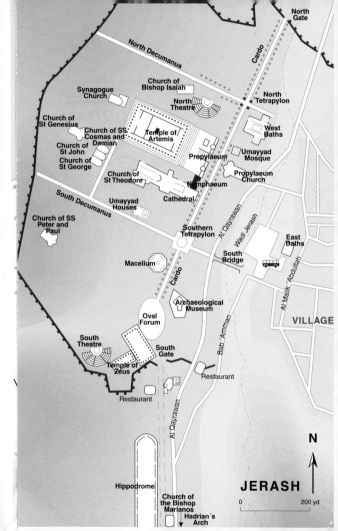

North Gate

North Decumanus

Cardo

Synagogue Church

Church of Bishop Isaiah

North Theatre

North Tetrapylon

Church of St Genesius

Church of SS Cosmas and Damian

Temple of Artemis

West Baths

Church of St John

Church of St George

Umayyad Mosque

Propylaeum

Church of St Theodore

Propylaeum Church

Cathedral

Nymphaeum

South Decumanus

Umayyad Houses

Church of SS Peter and Paul

Southern Tetrapylon

East Baths

South Bridge

Macellum

Cardo

Archaeological Museum

VILLAGE

Oval Forum

South Theatre

South Gate

Temple of Zeus

Restaurant

P

Al Qayrawan

Bab 'Amman

Wadi Jerash

Al Malik 'Abdullah

Restaurant

Hippodrome

Church of the Bishop Marianos

Hadrian's Arch

N

JERASH

0   200 yd

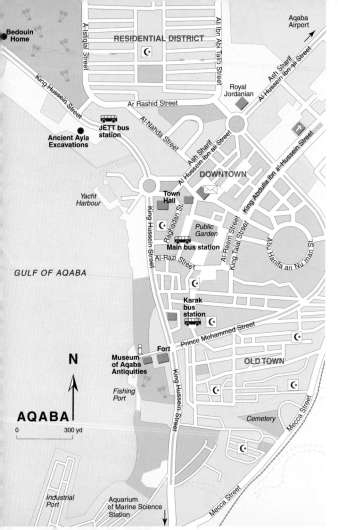